My Dream for a Good Life!

Ingrid De Michele

outskirts
press

Outskirts Press, Inc.
http://www.outskirtspress.com

ISBN: 978-1-9772-2449-1

I dedicate this book to my loving
mother and to all my siblings,
Renate, Hans, Helga and Freddy!

Table of Contents

Chapter 1	1
Chapter 2	4
Chapter 3	8
Chapter 4	12
Chapter 5	14
Chapter 6	17
Chapter 7	21
Chapter 8	23
Chapter 9	25
Chapter 10	28
Chapter 11	30
Chapter 12	32
Chapter 13	34
Chapter 14	38
Chapter 15	44
Chapter 16	48

Chapter 17	50
Chapter 18	53
Chapter 19	56
Chapter 20	59
Chapter 21	62
Chapter 22	65
Chapter 23	68
Chapter 24	71
Chapter 25	75
Chapter 26	77
Chapter 27	80
Chapter 28	82
Chapter 29	85
Chapter 30	88
Chapter 31	91
Chapter 32	94
Chapter 33	98
Chapter 34	101
Chapter 35	104
Chapter 36	108
Chapter 37	109
Chapter 38	114
Chapter 39	121

Chapter 40   127

Chapter 41   133

Chapter 42   144

Chapter 43   154

Chapter 44   166

Chapter 45   173

Chapter 47   182

Chapter 48   190

Chapter 1

THE YEAR WAS 1945 and it was a beautiful Day, but there was a War going on in Germany!

I was still very young, but I remember hearing sirens all around us and my Mother yelling, get your things together, we must leave the House and go for shelter.

My Oma Anna (Grandmother) and my Siblings are running around trying to decide what to bring. My Mother was preparing a bottle of Milk for me, because she does not know how long we will have to stay in the Bunker.

We left the house and saw other People running towards the park, when my Mother realized that she forgot my bottle on the Table. I was sitting in a Stroller and she told my Oma," take them to the Bunker, I will be there soon".

They were all running as fast as they could, because we still heard the sirens all around us and Bombs exploding. My Sisters and Brother were scared but I was just happy that someone was wheeling me. My Oma was nervous waiting for my Mother to return with the bottle.

I was only 2 Years old, but I remember how we all huddled together in the bunker with other people and waited until we heard it was safe to go back home.

Every time we had to go there, I remember being very afraid because the Bunker was dark and cold. I only wanted to be held be my Mother, which she did, and she always tried to assure us, that we all would be all right.

We did not always go to the bunkers in the park, sometimes we went to the cellar in our house with all our neighbors and there it was also very cold and dark.

There was no place to sit except on the hard-stone floor. One time when we finally were able to come out of the bunker we heard and saw that our neighbors house was damaged from a bomb and we were glad that it didn't touch our house. We lived on the top floor in a small apartment, which only had two bedrooms and a kitchen with a couch in it, and a little storage area. The bathroom was in the hallway which was also used by our neighbors.

My mother was so strong then, taking care of four children without any support from my father, because he was a soldier and away fighting in the war.

　　　　　　　　　　　　　　　INGRID DE MICHELE

There was lots of damage in our town and it was sad to walk through it and see all the damage the bombs had done. The biggest store in the center of town, which was located next to the big catholic church, was just a pile of rubble. I did not understand any of this being so young, all I thought, they were bad people who did this.

There was very little food in the stores, and I know it was hard for my mother to feed us all. My Oma was still working and sometimes she would bring food home.

Chapter 2

WHEN MY OMA was young, she worked and lived as a maid by a wealthy family who owned a toy factory?

They had a son who was interested in her and made her believe that he loved her and wanted to marry her. She became pregnant by him and when his family found out, they thought she was not good enough for their only son and fired her. They told her, not to expect any help from them, if she wants to keep the child.

So, she had to move back, and she gave birth to a baby girl (my mother) in February of 1914 in a town called Giesen and named her Emilie.

My Mother told me, that her family never made her feel bad that she was born out of wedlock and everybody loved her.

After her mother gave birth, she had to find another job. She became the servant of another rich family and they allowed her sometimes to bring her daughter to work, if she didn't have anyone to watch her. Mostly though my mother was raised by her grandparents!

My mother grew up in a time when Hitler was in power and she would tell me how much German people hated him. Lots of young people held demonstrations but had to be careful in what they did or said, otherwise they could be taken away and thrown into camps or be shot. She saw that happening to someone she knew, and she never saw them again. I could not imagine living in a time like that!

Well anyway, when my mother was a young lady she also worked in a household for families, which thought her how to cook, clean and take care of children.

She was 19 years old when she met my father who was a soldier. He was born in a city called Herne and that was the same region were my mother was born.His parents had moved though and bought a small farm, to a small village called Moosburg, which is a region of Bavaria.

He married my mother in 1935 and brought her to the village where is parents lived. It was a big change for her, and she told me that in the beginning she had a hard time there, she was not used to doing farm work.

Her in-laws were very old fashioned and stern people and my father was not very supportive to his new bride and left her alone many times.

I never met those grandparents on my fathers' side, because they already had passed away when I was born.

My mother gave birth to a baby girl the following year and they named her Renate.

My sister Renate would later tell me stories about the grandparents when I was older, but nothing special that I could remember.

After my mother was pregnant with her second child, they moved to a larger town called Erding and there my brother Hans was born in 1939. He would tell me, when he was a little boy my father would sometimes take him to visit his parents and that he loved that little farm.

Erding was not far away from Moosburg, only about 8 miles but it was a nice town with big stores.

My mother had another little girl in 1941, she named her Helga; she was born on April first. After that my father went to war again and he only came back for short leave's. I'm sure my mother and my siblings were happy to see him.

I was conceived when my father came home for another short leave during the war. He was not there when my mother gave birth to me, in February of 1943, and my name is Ingrid.

Every February, on the day before Ash Wednesday, is a big carnival celebration in Germany (called Fasching) and everyone is very happy and jolly. It was on such a day that I was born, and

I always considered myself to be special because I arrived on a such happy day!

After my father left the last time into the war, my mother never heard from him. She did not know if he was alive or dead, until he came home in 1946.

In the meanwhile, my mother was struggling to keep us all fed. She had very little money, only what she received from the government and there was no way she could go to work with four children at home.

My Oma had followed my mother when she got married and found a job at a big farm where she also lived, but she was able to help with food, that she received from her employer.

Chapter 3

My grandmother was a very bitter woman, not very loving and we always had to be in best behavior. My mother blamed it on the only man she loved who left her with his child, without offering support.

When I grew older, I always wondered how my mother became such a loving person, but I think it was because she was mostly raised by her grandparents, who loved her very much.

My mother kept all of us together, and she tried very hard to make us happy with whatever little she had.

We lived very close to the towns park, which was a place my older siblings always went to play and be with other children. There were just a few swings and a slide, but that was enough for them.

I know, my older sister Renate went to the park very often

after school and every time she came home, she was telling my mother, that there is a man in the park who played the accordion to entertain the children. She begged my mother to come with her to see him, but she was always busy and told her some other time. My mother had taking in laundry to be ironed, so she could earn extra money.

Renate didn't let up asking her to come to the park, so one day she gave in and went with her, wheeling me in the carriage and she met this man; his name was Erwin and they talked. After that she would go with Renate more often. As time went on, my mother and Erwin became friends and sometimes my mother would invite him to our house. He was a soldier far away from his family and he had a funny accent when he spoke, at least that's what my sisters and brother thought.

Erwin told my mother that his mother lived with his sister, which really was not his sister; (they found her on the doorsteps in front of their house) they were living in northern Germany, which became known as east Germany after the war, and he could not go back. That part of Germany was taken over by the Russians and he was afraid he would be captured and thrown in jail or killed if he tried.

Well, my mother became very fond of him and not having a man in her life for years and, not knowing if my father was alive or dead, she became involved with Erwin and became pregnant. He was at our house all the time. My stepbrother was born in august of 1946 and they named him Alfred.

The same year my father was released from a Russian prison,

where he was captured over three years ago. When he came home, he was very upset about Erwin and threw him out of the house and told my mother she cannot see him again and to give the baby away, to a home.

My sisters and brother where happy to have my father back home, but I did not know him so I can't say if I felt happy. The only man I knew was Erwin and now he was not there anymore.

My father was very sick and undernourished when he came back, so he was sent away to recuperate at a clinic in the mountains.

In this clinic he met a woman who was a nurse's aide and he became involved with her. She had a little girl and her husband had been killed in the war. When my father returned from the clinic, I was about four years old and I knew there was trouble in my house. My father was fighting with my mother all the time when he was at home and she cried a lot. That made me very sad; I did not like the fighting. It always made me think that nobody loved each other in our house.

It did not help that my father went out alone many times and came home drunk!

If all this was not bad enough, my mother never stopped seeing Erwin and found out that she was carrying Erwin's second child. When my father found out he told her, he would have excepted the first child, but he will not raise two children by another man, so they made the decision to divorce.

INGRID DE MICHELE

I think they both knew this was the best thing to do, because my mother did not want to leave Erwin and my father was the whole time this was going on, seeing his lady friend from the hospital. I found out later in life that my mother knew of this woman and that my father was never faithful while he was married to her.

I guess that is why it was not hard for her to leave my father.

She gave birth to Erwin's second child in January of 1949 and they named him Reinhardt, he was a precious little boy and they married in March of the same year.

My father also married the same year and moved with his new wife, her name was Amalie, to the other side of town. His wife was also expecting a child by him already, she gave birth in July of 1949. She left her little girl with her mother who raised her from birth, while she was working at the clinic.

Chapter 4

FROM THE MOMENT my mother married Erwin, my life and that of my siblings changed drastically. We did not see my father except my sister Renate, she chose to live with him when they divorced. She was already thirteen years old and she told my mother that she was not happy living in the same house with Erwin and that made my mother very upset.

Well, my mother had all to do to keep us together and raise us the right way, but from the moment they married he interfered very strongly. He thought she was too easy on us. We soon saw that he was not the kind of man we wanted for my mother, but sadly it was too late.

He wanted us to call him papa which was hard for my older siblings because they knew my father better then I. My brother Hans said to him once, I have a papa (father), which made him very mad and he had to suffer for it.

There was never enough money for food and my mother only received 25 deutsch marks for each child as child support, which was very little.

There was a kindergarten (preschool) not far from our house where the parents could drop of their children once they were potty trained, but we were never able to go there because there was a fee which my mother never had.

Whenever we passed by the garten there were always children playing and they seemed to have a good time and we wished, we were there with them.

When I was 6 years old, I started school. I was so excited because that meant I could learn, and the same time be out of the house most of the day. I could see how happy my siblings were when they were able to start school.

Living with my stepfather was not easy, there was always fighting going on I became a child who was always afraid, and my siblings felt the same. He was extremely strict with us; We had to do whatever he said otherwise he would beat us. We were not allowed to speak at the dinner table and if one of us would forget, he would hit us across the face or send us to bed without food. We always seemed to be in his way, and he wanted my mother's attention only for him alone. My mother had a tough time, but she was so blinded by love for him that she did not see what was happening to her children.

Chapter 5

MY BROTHER HANS was a loving boy and I was extremely close to him. He told me one day, Ingrid as soon as I can, I will move out and go to work and I did not want to think about that. It made me very sad.

My grandmother was no help, she had no patience with us, and she hated Erwin, because she saw how he manipulated my mother. She also was sick many times, in and out of the hospital.

When Erwin was at work my mother tried to give us love and told us it will get better, but that never happen because he was more out of work then working. We found out very quickly that he was a lazy man.

Many times, there was little food in the house, but my step-father always made sure he had enough for himself. With the food we did have my mother tried to make the best meals, she was an excellent cook even though it was simple, but everything tasted good. My stepfather liked rice soup with meat bones in it which made it very greasy. I hated that soup, but I had to eat it even though every time I did, it made me vomit and he would hit me for it. My mother was also a good baker and a great housewife. Our little apartment was always spotless even with so many people living there she always made sure it was clean; she always told us how important it is to have a clean house.

When she wasn't busy cooking or cleaning, we could see her sitting in the kitchen on the couch with knitting needles making something for one of us.

My house was very busy with five children and our grandmother in that small apartment.

My stepbrother Alfred was a little red-haired boy and he did not have it easy in his first years because everyone blamed him for splitting up my parents, but naturally it was not his fault.

Nobody wanted to play with him, but I always felt sorry for him. I can still see him crying, his nose running; calling someone and nobody paid attention.

Many times, there were other children in our yard, they were from other tenants who lived in the same house and they all did not like him. They also knew how mean his father was and how he treated us, and I think he had to suffer for it.

Reinhardt, the second child from my stepfather was a beautiful little boy. He was very quiet and learned quickly. My grand-mother adored him, and she took him many times to visit the family where she used to work.

My brother Hans, my sister Helga and I were very close and loved each other very much. I looked up to them and always begged them to play with me. When my brother had to go somewhere, I always wanted to go with him. We both liked to sing, and we always dreamed of becoming big stars.

When Helga was not in school, she had to help my mother a lot with the housework and take care of Reinhardt.

She would get mad at me when I tried to get away without doing my chores. Many times, she would tell my mother the reason I would eat so slow, was because I didn't want to help with the dishes, and she was right. I did not like housework, even though I had to do my share.

To this day I hate polishing shoes , because every Sunday my stepfather lined up all our shoes and I had to clean them and if he was not happy the way they looked, he would smack me on my head and I had to do them all over again.

Chapter 6

WE WERE HARDLY ever allowed to go out and play on Sunday afternoon, he made us stay home and help him work on old radio equipment that he found somewhere, and he wanted to fix them.

The house we lived in was a very large house. It had three stories, and on every floor, there lived two families. The owner lived on the main floor with her husband and a son of her sisters that she raised, because she could not have children of her own. They had a huge trucking/transport business.

The landlady was very mean and nasty she never had a nice thing to say about anybody.

She would constantly go to church and when she came back, she would yell and curse. There was a huge garden in the back of the house with many fruit trees and when she saw us in there she would run after us with a stick. She rather let the fruit from the trees rot on the floor, then give us some.

Sometimes she made my mother's life hell, especially when she was late with the rent which was quiet often because my stepfather was always out of work.

We lived on the top floor. We had no running water in the apartment, there was a sink on the outside hallway which we shared with the other tenant on the same floor. The same with the toilet, it also was in the hallway for both tenants to use. We had no heating in the apartment only a stove which we had to heat with wood or coal if we had money to buy it.

Many times, Hans and Helga had to go to the train station when we heard a coal train was coming, to see if they could find coal which fell of the train. When I got older, I had to do the same thing and it was heavy to carry home.

My stepfather was never satisfied when we didn't get enough.

There was a washhouse behind the house were everybody used to wash clothes. Every tenant had their day when to wash their clothes and if the weather was good, they could hang it on the lines outside or in bad weather up in the attic.

Every Friday or Saturday was bath day. In the summer we could go in the washhouse and take a bath and when it was cold outside my mother would fill a large tub and put it in the kitchen and all of us children would get a bath.

From the moment I understood my body, I realized, that every time we would bathe, my stepfather would always be in the same room, which Helga and I hated, but were too afraid to say anything to my mom.

INGRID DE MICHELE

We did not see our sister Renate very much; she did not come to visit because she hated Erwin. She was living with my father and when she turned fourteen years old, she started working for an American family.

There were lots of Americans living in my hometown. We had an air force base with lots of soldiers stationed there and many of the soldiers brought their families over from the united states.

Behind our house was a very nice area with large houses which were owned by mostly rich and businesspeople. They were all forced to vacate their homes and the soldiers who had a high rank moved in there with their families.

I became very friendly with a family who moved in there. They had a little girl my age and I had met her when we were playing outside. Her name was Caroline and she invited me often to her house. She had lots of toys which I had never seen.

I thought I was so special the way her family treated me, and I loved going there. They always served good food and there was never any yelling, her parents were very happy people.

I learned to speak a little English and sometimes I pretend that they were my family and I told myself" if I can't take it any-more at home I would make them take me to America", but deep down I knew I would never leave my mother!

They took me many times to the px, which was a store on the base and only American soldiers could shop there. In the store they had things I never seen before, but mostly I was interested in the different kind of chocolate bars they sold. I loved eating chocolate, but we never got any except maybe a little on Christmas. Caroline's parents always let me pick one and I was a happy girl.

My stepfather wanted to know what I did there, but I never told him where they take me. I would say, we only play with her toys and she had so many. Sometimes they took me to their church on Sundays, even though I did not understand what they were saying. I was happy that my mother allowed me to go because after church they would invite me sometimes to stay for dinner and I never seen so much food.

Caroline's mother always made sure we had enough before she served her husband and her; not like in my house, we had to wait and see that my stepfather had enough for himself first.

By spending so much time with Caroline as possible, I was able to learn more English and I could speak to them better. My whole family learned a little English because there were always so many Americans everywhere. We found out that the town was going to build a whole neighborhood right outside the base where only Americans could live.

Chapter 7

AT HOME THINGS did not get any better. My mother became very sick and she had to go to the hospital for surgery. She was in there 4 weeks and for that time there was hell at home. I did not have much time to spend with Caroline and that made me very sad.

My stepfather was again out of work and for us to eat he would send us to the local hospital with a metal milk can and made us beg for leftover food. I was mortified and embarrassed and I tried to hide behind my sister Helga, so nobody recognizes me: but they already knew who we were. If we did not go, there would be nothing to eat that night.

The other things I hated which he made us do, was on January 6th which was the holiday of the three kings, we had to dress up in a white sheet and paint our face either red or brown and go from house to house and hope the people would give us anything. It was a custom many other poor kids also did, but I hated it.

People would give us all kinds of things, like eggs, apples, oranges, cookies and sometimes money, but never much. Even before Easter, he would send us to the farmers and beg for eggs, he would sometimes spy on us to see if we would eat anything, before we brought it home: at least that is what he told us and we believed him. Every year before Christmas he told us, that he would not allow my mother to buy a Christmas tree, but my mom always brought one home anyway on Christmas eve.

So, when we saw a tree, we knew it was my mother's doing, she did not want us to be sad. Before Christmas my mom would bake all kinds of delicious cookies and she would hide them, but my sister knew where and she always sneak into the closet to get some.

There would never be a lot of presents for us, almost every year we would get new underwear, which we needed and a tray of goodies with cookies, some chocolate and oranges. There was never a toy maybe some marbles to play with and some colored pencils for school.

INGRID DE MICHELE

Chapter 8

ALL THE TIME my mother was in the hospital, I was not allowed to go to Caroline's house and I was very unhappy. I was glad when my mom came home, but she needed help with everything which was okay with me, I was just happy to have her back home and not be alone with him.

At that time, I had a problem in school, but not with learning. My problem was that I used to get urinary trac infections which was painful, and it made me wet my pants many times. My teacher would send me home with a note to tell my mom that she should take me to the doctor, but my stepfather thought it was all in my head and he refused to let my mom take me to have it checked out. When I finally went to the doctor, I needed a procedure to make it better.

It was now 1952 and my stepfather finally got a job. My brother Hans was very unhappy at home and I know he went to visit my father many times. He had one more year in school then he would need to go to work. I was not looking forward for that!

My baby brother Reinhardt was a pleasure to have around. He was very lovable, and he was getting so smart for his age, he was like a little man. One day on a hot day in June of 1952, my grandmother wanted to visit the family she used to work for. It was a holiday weekend (Pfingsten), she asked my mother if she could take Reinhardt with her because he loved riding on a bus. My mom said okay and the rest of us could go to the town swimming pool, so she can have time for herself. We loved going to the swimming pool, it was close to our house and we were able to walk there alone. Hans was already thirteen years old, so my mother told him to watch us. That was funny because Helga and I loved to swim, and Hans hated to go in the water. We all met neighborhood kids there and had lots of fun.

After my grandmother came back from her trip, Reinhardt wanted to go to the pool to be with us. Helga had gone home to get something, and she took him back with her. We all had to watch him, he always wanted to be with us in the big pool instead of the shallow pool, but there were too many people and kids jumping around.

Chapter 9

~

AFTER A WHILE he got tired and wanted to go back home. Usually he would nap in the afternoon, which he did not do today, so I took him home and went back to the pool. My mom told us we had to be home by 6pm, which we did because we were afraid to be late if my stepfather would be home.

When we got home, my mother asked us where Reinhardt was, and we all answered he is home. My mom got very nervous when my grandmother told her that she let him go back to the pool by himself. She told him to look for us, but we never saw him come back.

We all started crying, my stepfather became outraged and we all ran back to the swimming pool to look for him. When we got there and told the pool attendants, they made everyone get out of the pool and started the search. Some of the people who were there also looked for him on the grounds and in the shallow pool but no luck. By this time my mom was getting hysterical and several people tried to comfort her. All of us were so scared we could not believe my grandmother let him go to the pool without telling us. Hours went by and they decided to drain the big pool and to do so they had to open the locks.

One person noticed that the handle on the lock was turned towards the outside and it had should have been on the inside. Many older kids played with the handle to open the lock to let more water into the pool.

Well, when they saw that the handle was turned, they wanted to inspect the reservoir of the lock and when they did, they saw a little body floating. When they took it out it was my little brother? Someone called the doctor who was already at the pool to perform life savings methods, but it was too late; he was in the water too long. When they told my mom, she collapsed, but she heard the doctor make a comment" I don't know why she is so upset, she has 5 other children". She never forgave him for that remark! All us couldn't believe that little Reinhardt was dead.

My grandmother was very upset and blamed herself for letting Reinhardt go to the pool by himself. After the funeral, which was a terrible ordeal, my house became unbearable. My mom became withdrawn and cried a lot, all of us were afraid to talk to her, she walked around like a zombie.

My grandmother had told my mom sometime later what Reinhardt had said on the day he died. When they were on the bus that morning on their way back, apparently the bus was going a little too fast and he said "Oma if this bus doesn't slow

INGRID DE MICHELE

down, we all going to die". It's like he knew his life was coming to an end, naturally this was no comfort to my mom.

It took my mom about six months to become herself again, but there was always sadness in her eyes and she never mentioned Reinhardt.

I never gave my mother any problems and always listen to her, but now I tried to be especially good and do everything my mom said and my brothers and sister did to.

We were all in school during the day, so my mom only had her mother at home with her. My stepfather became unbearable to live with, I think he blamed all of us for the dead of his son and many times when he was mad at us, which was very often, he would tell us so. We were not able to play outside and we had to come home right after school.

Chapter 10

I LOVED SCHOOL and wished we had to go all day because there, I was the happiest. Sometimes we had sewing and knitting classes after school which I also loved, and my brother Hans also went to the knitting class because the teacher always had peanut butter from her American friends, and she made us sandwiches which we liked. On most Sundays we had to stay in the house and help my stepfather with his stupid hobbies of fixing old radios. I hated helping him, because he had no patience and got mad at us when things didn't go his way.

He expected me to know all the tools I was supposed to hand him and when I gave him the wrong one, he would hit me across the face.

In the later part of the same year my grandmother got sick again. I remember she had a huge sore on her leg that would not heal, and she had trouble getting around. I was very young and did not understand the reason for that. All I know my stepfather was happy whenever she was in the hospital; he would say "one less mouth to feed".

With my stepfather never having a good job, there was never enough money in our house and many times we were sent to the market to buy food without money. We had to tell the store owner to but it on our bill and hoped he would do it. There were times when he said, tell your mother no more credit! As young as I was, I knew that was not the way to live and became embarressed and shy. I always felt people would know how poor we were!

It seemed my stepfather had money for everything else except for putting food on the table and other necessities. We never had anything new to wear, only hand me downs.

When there was money, we were sent every 2 or 3 weeks to the town slaughterhouse to buy meat. We had to get up very early, like 4 am on Saturday morning and stand online for the meat. In the winter it was so cold that we could not stand outside, so we went into the stables where the cattle were kept before they were slaughtered. We would lay on the hay on the opposite side to keep warm. It stunk so bad in there, but we had to stay in there until the selling of the meat started. I still remember how bad I felt for the cows when I saw what they did to them.

We were the only children who were there and some of the other people could not understand that our parents would send us there. I know my mother did not like us going there, but she was not able to say anything to her husband because he would get to angry and she tried to keep piece in the family. He also told her we had to earn our food and she shouldn't feel bad.

Chapter 11

THE FOLLOWING YEAR 1953 my brother Hans turned 14 and he was finished with school. He had a hard time in school and learning did not come easy for him especially in reading. He wanted to learn a trade, but my stepfather wanted him to work on a farm because he was able to live there.

Even though Hans was happy to get out of the house he did not like working on a farm. He was upset that our father did nothing to help him find better work. Our father never checked on us to see how we were raised or how we were doing. He never invited us to his house when we were little. I think my stepfather would not have let him in the house. There were times when we saw our father on the street when my stepfather was with us, he made us go on the other side and we could not say anything to him.

My father had a daughter and a son with his second wife and a good job on the base. He also made extra money selling insurance, so his family lived much better than us.

The farm where Hans worked was about five miles away and I was sad because I missed him terribly. He would come home sometimes on weekends but then he had little time for me, after all he was a young man and didn't always wanted his little sister tagging along.

Our life did not change a great deal. My mom still grieved for little Reinhardt and she had a hard time getting back to a normal life until I started to get sick.

I was constantly getting bad stomach pains until my mom finally took me to the doctor to have me checked out. There were not many doctors in our town, so she had to take me to the same one who made that bad remark when little Reinhardt died. He told her that I had a cold in my stomach, and it should go away.

Chapter 12

⁓

MANY TIMES, I could not go to school because the pain was so strong, and it made me vomit. My stepfather was mad at me and told me that I was faking it and send me to school anyway.

Finally, he had gotten a job where he had to take a train to get there. One day when he came home, he told my mother that he met a very nice man on the train, and he belonged to this religion and he wanted to invite him to our house. So, they did and when the man came, he told them all about this new religion and how all the members helped each other. Well, my stepfather said he would take all of us to this church for the next service to check it out .All of us children were raised by my mother in the Lutheran religion and I and my siblings did not want to go to a new church, but we had no choice in this matter.

We all went to this church every Sunday and as the weeks past we realized that the people from the church were very nice to all of us, and my Stepfather talked my mother into joining. The only thing I liked about this church was, that I was able to join the choir. I liked to sing, and they would let me sing alone and that made me feel good.

I saw very soon that my stepfather took totally advantage of those nice people and we did not like it.

I still was not feeling any better and one Sunday when we were at church, I had gotten severe pains in my stomach again. The people in the church told my mother she should take me to the hospital but my stepfather thought it was not necessary, but as the pain got worse he said he would take me and I know he only did it, to show the people there that he was a concerned parent which he always did just to impress them.

I was so grateful to them because if they wouldn't have insisted to take me to the hospital, I could have died according to the doctor, because my appendix had ruptured, and I was very sick.

Chapter 13

I WAS IN the hospital for two weeks and one day when I was allowed to get up, I was standing by my bed when I slipped back, and my stitches opened and I was bleeding badly. They had to stitch me back up again.

The next day when I woke up my bed was full of blood again and I got scared, I thought my stitches did not hold. When the nurse came in to check me out, she asked me if this had happened to me before, but I didn't know what she meant.

While she cleaned me up, she explained to me that there was nothing to worry about and that I was probably going to have this every month. I was very confused and when my mom came to visit, she was very surprised that I already started my monthly period. My sister Helga was two years older than me and this did not happen to her yet.

Naturally my mother told my stepfather and he made stupid

remarks when I got home, and I was so embarrassed. He would always look at me in a curious way and I did not like it and he still insisted that we would bath in the kitchen where he was present. I told my mother that I did not want to do that anymore and she let us bath in the washhouse then. I did not care how cold it was in there.

I did not trust my stepfather because whenever I happen to be close to him, he would always touch me in a way I thought was wrong. One time he brushed with his hands down my growing breast and I told him if he ever did that again I would tell on him. He got mad at me, like I was doing something wrong.

Later I found out that he also touched my girlfriend's breast and he would hug her when she would come to my house. After that none of my friends wanted to visit me if he was at home.My sister Helga said the same happen to her. We couldn't tell my mom; she would have never believed us and if he would have found out he would hurt us.

Now, that I was a little older I could go with my sister Helga to the park to play. One day we decided to go there and instead of just playing on the swings, we walked around and visited the zoo in the park. In there, were deer and goats and little pony's, also beautiful peacocks and smaller animals. When we had to start going back home, we decided to go a different way, which I didn't like, it was a little too scary for me, but my sister held my hand. As we walked along the path, we saw something strange on a tree and it turned out, that it was a man who hung himself. We couldn't believe what we saw and ran home to tell our mother. She almost did not believe us, but the next day she heard it when she went to town. I never went that way again, when I was in the park!

One day my mother told us that she and my stepfather decided that they would like to have another child to replace Reinhardt. We could not understand that because we had so little room and not much to eat, why bring another child into this house. Naturally we had nothing to say about that.

My stepbrother Alfred (we called him Freddy) slept in a small bed in my mother's bedroom. My sister Helga and I slept in one bed, she on top and me on the bottom. My grandmother slept in the same small room as us, it was very tight. There was not even a door to close the room, there was only a curtain to block out the light.

My mom became pregnant very soon and she was to give birth in the summer. She did not have an easy pregnancy and when she was in her seventh month, she told us that she couldn't feel the baby move. When she went to the doctor, he told her that could happen sometimes, but not to worry. My mother did not think everything was alright, but she hoped otherwise. One day, while I was walking with her to town, she started bleeding and the blood was all black. She collapsed on the street and I got very scared, thinking that she would die.

I ran to get help and thank god there was a doctor nearby who called an ambulance immediately and brought her to the hospital. I had to run home and tell my stepfather what happened, and he went to the hospital.

INGRID DE MICHELE

My mom was very sick, they had to operate and take the baby from her, which was already dead in her belly and all her insides were poisoned. They had to perform a hysterectomy and they told my stepfather there will be no more children. Again, my mother was very sad, and it hurt me to see her that way. I could not understand why god made her suffer so much and I wished I could make things better for her.

Chapter 14

I CONSTANTLY THOUGHT about the bad things in our life and I wanted my life to change, the only thing that made me happy was that I was able to go to school or I was able to spend time with Caroline again, which wasn't that often anymore. Even that was going to change soon, because her father told me they were going to go back to America real soon.

There was never happiness or much love going around in our house and sometimes I would dream that when I got older, I would work very hard to make lots of money, so I can take my mom away from this man she married.

I did not know that my mother loved this man no matter what he did, to this day I cannot understand how she could have loved him! He was a very selfish man and only thought of himself and made her life miserable.

My sister Renate hardly ever came by and I know that hurt my mother, but she hated my stepfather even though it was her fault that my mom met him.

Also, my brother Hans stayed away more, and I missed him a lot.

I was now 10 years old and I was doing well in school. I was happy to have the same teacher I had in 3rd grade. When I left her class at the end of that school year, I was happy that I knew I would have my teacher in the following year again and she wished as a good summer.

Our summers were never that special, we never went anywhere. I always tried to have friends come over to play with us, but we did not have that many friends and most did not like to come because of my stepfather. Some of the children did not want to play with us because we were poor. When some friends did come, we would always play school and I had to be the teacher, because that is what I wanted to be when I grew up.

When the summer was over I was excited to be going into 4th grade to see my teacher again, she understood my problems at home and told me many times "Ingrid you can come to me anytime if you want to talk,' but I think she knew that I couldn't do that. If my stepfather would have found out that I complained to someone, god knows what he would have done. I also wouldn't want to hurt my mom!

Just to have a teacher offer me help made me feel better. She was a special lady. She came from royal blood. She lived with her two daughters, which were real princesses and the younger one was in my class, in a small castle near my hometown. It was owned by her husband who died in the war, that is why she had to work. The town was even named after her (Fraunberg). She invited me many times to come to her house, but I never had a chance to go there. Who would have brought me there anyway?

I was happy that I still had my friend Caroline to play with, but one day in the spring of 1954 she told me that her family were finally going back to America and she wanted me to come and be her sister. Her dad even asked my mother if she would consider letting me go with them. He knew our circumstances at home, and he told her he could give me a much better life with lots of opportunities. His family would take good care of me and love me like a daughter and Caroline would have a sister. His wife was not able to have more children.

It made my mother cry and she thanked them, but she could never give me away. I was sad to see Caroline leave and cried many days, but I knew I would have not gone with her, no matter how bad it was at home, I could not leave my mother.

Right after Caroline left my mom found out about a program where poor children could be sent away for the whole summer. The girls would be taken in by a family and the boys would go to a camp. Just before the school year was over, we found out that my sister Helga and I, and my brother Freddy were chosen, and we were very excited. We had never been away and the thought of not seeing my stepfather for the whole summer was great. It made me also feel better about Caroline leaving.

INGRID DE MICHELE

I wrote her a letter right of way, to tell her, so she would know that I would be away the whole summer. When it was the end of the schoolyear, I was sad to leave my teacher but she told me" Ingrid don't ever forget who you are and work very hard, then better times will come", and she wished me a great summer!

A week after school ended in July of 1954 my mother was packing our suitcases which we had to borrow from someone, and she brought us to the people who oversaw our trip. My mom was a little sad to see us go but my stepfather kept telling her, it would be good for them, she would have more time for him!

We were taken by train, which we loved because we never been on one, to east Germany, to a city called Berlin. It was a long ride and it was night when we arrived. Then were taken by bus to a camp where we stayed overnight. We were very tired, and I was scared about being away from home and I missed my mother. I was glad though, I had my sister Helga with me, she was so much more stronger than me. My brother Freddy was never scared, he thought it was great to be away.

The following day, after having a delicious breakfast, which we never had before in our life, we had to get on a truck, sitting on benches on either side. They told us that they wanted to show us the city and then drive us to meet the families where we going to stay. We drove almost all day through Berlin and then to Dresden and we were shocked of what we saw.

Most of the city was bombed and in rubbles from the war. There were piles of broken stone where buildings used to stand. We passed a church; part was still standing but the bell tower was lying on top of some walls. There were Trees growing out of the piles of stones. I had never seen anything like this in my life, and all the children on the truck were scared and cried. It was much worse, then when my hometown was bombed, but this was a much larger city. Our chaperone told us we should not be afraid, that we were old enough to understand what the war did, and we should tell our families and teachers what we saw.

Well, after we drove through the bombed -out city we came to an area of Dresden which was rebuild after the war. Our chaperone explained that they were marking and saving all the stones and bricks because eventually they would rebuild this beautiful city, the way it was. I could not imagine that this could be possible. They said right now they just needed housing for the people who lived there.

Dresden was known for its richness, it had a castle surrounded by this huge wall with great statues on them, it was called the Zwinger! We were told that there were many paintings by famous artist, but they were able to hide them before the Russians could get their hands on them. The city was also known for the Dresden china. They took us to the factory where they made the china and it was something to see and I wished I would have been able to buy a small piece of souvenir and bring it to my mother. Even that factory was damaged by the war, but it was already restored.

(I was able to go back to Dresden after the wall came down with my husband and I was amazed how they had restored the city; it was beautiful. It brought back many memories!)

We did not meet the families we stayed with until late that evening. Helga and I had to say goodbye to Freddy when they dropped the boys of at the camp. We were assured that we would see him during our vacation, because they had trips scheduled for all the children.

As soon as I met the family I was going to stay with, I felt very comfortable. Their name was Boehme, they were very nice. They took me to their home where I met the rest of the family, there was a 15-year-old daughter named Gitta and an 11-year-old girl named Ingrid, like me. They also had a 6-year-old son named Peter. I was so happy that Ingrid was my age, so I had someone to play with. Her mother decided to call me Inge, so we would not get confused when she called us.

First, I had a hard time understanding them because they spoke a much different dialect then me, but it did not take me long and I started to speak just like them. They were amazed how easy it came to me, but I was always good at picking up other dialects.

They owned their own home with a huge garden to play in. There were all kinds of fruit trees, apples, pears, and plums, it was great, and I could pick as much as I liked, without getting in trouble.

Chapter 15

BESIDES HAVING THREE meals a day was a treat by itself. They also had a television which I had never seen before, plus a bed of my own to sleep in, I was in heaven. I thought these people must be rich and I was a lucky girl for coming to their home.

The town they lived in was called Ottendorf-Okrilla it was very small, and we were able to walk all over without getting lost. I did not know what kind of job Herr Boehme had but he left early in the morning and came home late at night.

So many times, I did not see him all week. On the weekends he was always home, and he did different things with us.

The same time I met my new family, my sister Helga met hers and we were happy to find out they lived in the same town. The man was even the mayor of the town and he had a beautiful house, but they were already a little older and had no children which made Helga a little sad. She was aloud though to come and visit me anytime or meet us in town. The stores in town were very small and there was not much merchandise to buy, which I found strange.

Later I asked why that was and I was told, being this was east Germany everything was cut off from the westside and the only time the store would get new merchandise, is when the Russian Government allowed anything to come across the borders.

The people were not allowed to complain openly about this, because they could have been taken away. So when the people were out, they always spoke very quietly because the Russian soldiers were everywhere.

There were announcements when special things arrived at the stores, then everyone waited on long lines to get something.

They did not care what it was, anything would be good. One time I asked to come along and we waited in line for 7 hours to get oranges and bananas. I was astonished that these beautiful people who still lived in Germany, where divided and had to live this way.

They told me they were used to this kind of living and they were not bitter, because this was their home and they had to make the best of it. There was even a barb wire fence along the outskirts of the town, you were not allowed to come within 100 feet of it otherwise you could be shot.

To me it was still better than my own house and I was happy to be there, and I never heard any fighting and yelling going on.

I was always together with Ingrid and after we did our chores, we had plenty of time to play. We went on trips and Helga came with us. We also met up with our brother Freddy . We went hiking in the mountains, took boat rides and went to see a big zoo, we all were very happy.

Sometimes we went to fairs, there were lots of Russian soldiers walking around watching the people, but we were able to speak to some of them. They even tried to teach us their language, I learned some words while I was there but don't remember them anymore.

I had such a great time with my new family, I felt I belonged there, and they treated me like their own. As the time with them was coming to an end, they told me, if the program would allow it, they would take me in again next year, but my mother would have to register us as soon as possible.

The same was with Helga's family and Freddy and we all hoped it would happen.

We finally had to say goodbye and there were lots of tears. I couldn't thank them enough for all they did for me and I had to promise to write. My adopted family brought us to the meeting point, and we were all transferred to the train station after we picked up the children from the camp.

The trip home took all day and my mother was at the station in my hometown when we arrived, we were all happy to see her again. She asked us how we liked our vacation and we told her everything we did. All of us had different stories and we told

INGRID DE MICHELE

her to register us again for next year because they would take us again and my mom said she would.

Chapter 16

⌁

ONE WEEK LATER the new school year started and now I was in 5th grade. We had a new teacher; his name was Mr. Reiser. he was known to be a real history buff. Many children did not like him, but I had lots of things to tell him about my trip and he spoke about it all year. We were getting bored with his teaching! He was supposed to teach all subjects, but all he was interested in, was history and war. We were all wondering how he became a teacher. We were going to have him also for the 6th grade and we were not looking forward to it.

All the teachers at that time tought to grades, and as I said earlier that I liked Frau von Fraunberg, my 3rd and 4th grade teacher, the best because she understood me and liked me. Every time she saw me, she asked me how I was doing?

Now I also had lessons in the afternoon, I learned how to cook, sew and knit and that was exciting because it kept me in the school longer. We could have gone home for lunch but most of the time Helga and I stayed and ate the lunch my mother made us. The teacher who tought us knitting, still gave us peanut butter sandwiches and we loved them. My sister Helga was two years ahead of me, but she also had lessons in the afternoon.

Sometimes we went to our friend Marlina's house; she lived in a wooden barracks. It was very simple, there were only refugees from east Germany living there and she lived there with her mother in two rooms. She was a girl who sometimes came with us when we dressed up on three Kings day and went from house to house to get whatever people gave us.

Chapter 17

ONE DAY MY sister Renate told us that she was going to the movies with a few American soldiers she had met. She said that they wanted to meet us. We asked our mother and she let us go.

We were sitting in the row before her and one of the soldier his name was Mike, but they called him Pasquale, he constantly tapped my sister Helga on the shoulder and asked her to come sit with him, but Helga did not want to go, she was still too young.

A few months later Renate told us that she was dating Mike and she brought him to our house to meet my mother. He was very nice and handsome. Sometimes when he came to our house with Renate, they would bring his buddies along. My stepfather liked when they came to our house because they would always bring things from the px, the store on the base.

I don't remember all their names except one and that was

Robbie. He was nice to me, like an older brother and I liked him a lot. He would always bring me little presents. I had very straight hair and one day when he came; he asked my mother if she would take me to the hairdresser for a perm. He wanted to see my hair with curls, and he offered to pay for it; so, my mother accepted the money and took me the next day; I sure looked different.

When he came the next day, he brought me a brand-new dress in light blue, and it had pretty lace on it. It was the most beautiful dress I ever seen and owned and when I put it on, I felt like a princess and it fit me well. I wore that dress every Sunday when I could go out, until I grew out of it.

Sometimes my stepfather got jealous, especially when Robbie brought me things and nothing for him. He accused me of doing things to Robbie that I didn't even understand what he was talking about. He was always looking to get something from everyone.

Mike would tell us about his family who lived in Brooklyn New York.

He had two older sisters, Rose and Millie and a younger brother named Jack. He showed as pictures of them and he would always tease me about his younger brother.

That same year he was going home for Christmas and we all took him to the train station to say goodbye. While we were waiting for the train he asked me if he should give his brother a message from me and I told him, tell him, one day I will come to America and marry him, they all laughed and he said he would tell him!

I never told him, that I had taken a picture from him and cut out his brothers face and kept it in a safe place. When I got an I.D. bracelet for my birthday, I put the picture of Jack in there. His friend Robbie told me that he would take me to America when he gets out of the service, but I knew that would never happen.

INGRID DE MICHELE

Chapter 18

WHEN MIKE CAME back from America, he and Renate became
very serious with each other and he asked her to marry him.
She said yes but his Sargent would not allow it because he was
still very young.

My stepfather and mother spent a lot of time in that new
church, they had joined. I have to say the people were very
nice and the head preacher came many times to our house and
brought us things we needed, and I saw how my stepfather was
using him. My siblings and I were the whole time receiving
religious instructions in school and my stepfather told us to
tell the teacher that we will not participate anymore, but they
needed it in writing.

As I said earlier the only thing, I enjoyed at the church, was the
singing. I always thought I had a good voice and my brother
Hans too and we were always dreaming that we are going to
become big stars one day. We would make lots of money, then

take care of our mother the way she deserved, without my stepfather.

Every time Hans was home, we would hide somewhere to practice, and I loved it. These were short years and we soon realized it would never happen. We didn't know how to follow our dream and we had no one to help us.

As Hans got older, he did not come home so frequently, because every time he came home my stepfather would find a reason to fight.

He wanted Hans to give him the little money he made and always asked him, why he didn't bring us any meat or eggs, being he was working on a farm. Hans hated him and my mother knew it, but it hurt her anyway!

So, the year was almost over, and we had another one of our sad Christmases.

Right after new year we had a big snowstorm. The snow was so high that we could not get out of the front door. We were able to touch the snow from our kitchen window and we lived on the second floor. There was a shed attached to the back of the house under our window and we wanted to jump out and slide into the backyard if we would have been able to get back in the house, but that was impossible.

Two days after the snowfall our landlord decided to open the front door. We were all in the hallway on the steps and as he opened the front door slowly, the force of the heavy snow came in so quick and covered the entire hallway and the landlord had to dig himself out. For us kids, it was lots of fun to watch, all the men helped shuffling the snow out of the house and make a path to the street so we could get out.

We had to go back to school and walk in this heavy snow, it was a long walk to school, and we froze. Sometimes you couldn't even see me and Freddy because I was not tall, and Freddy was only 8 years old. It was lots of fun playing in the snow, but we were always cold because we did not have very warm clothes. We were glad when spring came again, and it was easier to play outside.

Chapter 19

IN MARCH OF 1955 my grandmother started to get sick again. My mother was very worried about her and finally she had to go back to the hospital where she was diagnosed with breast cancer. They had to remove both of her breasts; she was in the hospital for a long time.

Just before the end of the school year my mom was informed that we were able to go back to east Germany again and be with the same families. Helga was especially happy because this was her last summer before she had to find a job and she already had one waiting for her.

We left right after school ended and I was happy to see my adopted family again. We had kept in touch with letters, so I knew what happened in the past year. I was surprised when I saw Ingrid, she had really grown a lot and I was still short.

We were able to go on more trips to different places, but I was just happy to be with them. My brother Freddy went again to a camp and he also had a good time there.

One time it was already late at night when Herr Boehme told me that there was something, he wanted to show me, but I had to promise, that I would not tell anyone, because it would be very bad.

I was always good in keeping secrets and I told him so.

With a flashlight he took all the children outside in the dark; we crossed the garden and went into the garage and up a staircase holding hands. Once we were inside the room, he switched on a dim light and told us to stay against the wall. The windows were all blocked off so no light would come in or out.

He walked over to the other side and pulled on a chain and down from the ceiling came a very large platform in the size of the floor. There was a whole set-up of miniature trains with a big city and more than one train set on it. He told me that he builds this all by himself when he was a young man and the reason, they could only play with it at night was, there would be less danger for anyone to come around. He said if the Russian soldiers would find out, they would take it away and he would be in trouble. I had never seen anything like it, and we could stay there for hours and play.

The summer flew by and my time with them was coming to an end. I was so sad because I knew I would probably never see them again. They were only aloud to have the same children twice, but we promised to keep in touch as we did before. There were lots of tears when I left, and I was glad to have many pictures to remember them. I told them if it was ever possible in my life, that I would try to come and see them again.

(Which I was able to do much later in my life, with my husband.)

Chapter 20

WHEN WE GOT home, my mother was waiting for us at the train station. I noticed right away that something had happened because she looked very sad. She told us that our grandmother had died 2 weeks ago, but she didn't want to spoil our last days.

My mom said that our grandmother became very ill and she had to go back to the hospital. Her cancer had spread to her throat and she could not eat anymore. She said it was better that god took her, so she won't have to suffer anymore.

We all went to the cemetery the next day and visited the grave she now shared with her beloved grandson Reinhardt.

Well, Helga was now 14 years old and had to start working. Helga was not very happy at her job because my stepfather made her except this job in a family household, so she would have to live there. She had to do all the cleaning, cooking and laundry and sometimes she had to help at the butcher shop they owned. She told my mother that they made her work very hard, sometimes for 14 hours and they didn't even have a normal bed for her to sleep in. It was against the law to make a 14-year-old work that many hours, but she was afraid to do anything about it.

The only thing she liked, was that she was away from my stepfather, just like Hans!

For me, a new school year started and now I was in 6th grade still with Mr. Reiser as my teacher. I couldn't wait until the year was over, but that won't be for a while. The only thing I enjoyed was my sewing, knitting and cooking classes.

Now that I was the only girl at home, I had more chores to do and my stepfather made sure that I did them well.

I still had to polish all our shoes that he lined up every Sunday, which I hated to do, because if they were not to his satisfaction, I had to clean them all over again, after he hit me and called me names.

In the spring of 1956, I was supposed to make my confirmation in the new church. All the girls were supposed to wear a nice black dress, but my stepfather refused to buy me one. He said he had no money for it and told my mother she should see if we could borrow one. I was very upset because I never had a new dress except the one Robbie bought me; this was supposed to be an important day in my life!

Not until a few days before the event, my mother took me to

the store and bought me a dress. She would always put a little money in a hiding place for such occasions and I had to promise never to say anything to anyone. I would have never done that anyway and I loved my mother so much at that moment! That was also the way she was able to buy us little Christmas presents every year!

Before we came home with the dress, my mom removed all the tags and wrinkled the dress and told her husband that we borrowed the dress from someone she knew.

I was so grateful to her and happy. It was always hard for her when my stepfather was like that, because I know she wanted us to have a better life and it was difficult for her to make changes without making him mad.

I loved her even more for that!

Chapter 21

IT WAS A nice dress and on the day of my confirmation my mom fixed my hair and I felt very pretty. It was a sunny day and after the ceremony we all sat in the back yard and ate the beautiful cake my mother made. There wasn't anybody else there from my family, only Freddy and that made me a little sad.

Most of the kids who made their confirmation with me, told me that they were having a party with their whole families. My own father did not acknowledge my confirmation, because he did not like the church I belonged, but that did not surprise me, he was never much in our life anyway. My other siblings didn't want to come because of my stepfather, he was always looking for a fight and so they stayed away!

I kept in touch with Caroline and told her everything new in my life which was not much. I always had to write the letter for her in school and then ask my mother to mail it for me. One-time I wrote at home and my stepfather saw it and ripped it up, because he did not like what it said. When I received a letter from her, I would make Renate's boyfriend Mike translate it what I couldn't understand.

I also kept in touch with my second family in Ottendorf-Okrilla and I always received an answer from them, which made me very happy. They told me that their older daughter Gitta got engaged and they sent me a picture of the happy couple.

A few months after that, I received another letter from Frau. Boehme and she told me that she could not write me anymore, because they were moving and could not tell me where to. She wished me lots of luck in my life and told me to stay true to myself and it made me very sad. I thought at that time that they would try to escape over the border and then I would her from them again.

Many families still tried to escape the hard life of east Germany to have a better life in the west. It was very dangerous though and many people got caught and thrown in prison or shot.

I don't know what happen to the Boehme's, until much later in my life!

Well, the years were passing fast and I was going to my last year of school before I had to go to work. Since my sister had to go into a household, I told my mother I wanted to learn how to become a hairstylist. I always loved fixing my friends hair and made sure my own hair looked good.

Every year the stores and businesses in my hometown and

around the area notified the schools how many children they would take to teach them a trade. So, most of the kids in the eighth grades, knew what they wanted to be and applied for the job. You had to start about a half a year before the school year was over, otherwise all the openings would be filled.

I kept reminding my mother that I had to go to the beauty salons for an interview, but my stepfather had other ideas. He wanted me also to go to work in a household so I would be moving out.

Chapter 22

I REFUSED TO do that because Helga was not happy, and she also wanted to become a hairstylist and now she is stuck in a place she does not like.

My stepfather gave me a hard time; I told him that I would run away before I would work in a household. I had very good grades in school, that I could have continued my schooling but there was naturally no money for that and again I could not go to my father. Therefore, my stepfather made me miss all the opportunities to get a position as a hairdresser. Now there were only two more jobs available in my hometown, one was in a butcher shop which I refused to go and the other was learning to become a salesperson in an electrical store, so I took that, but was not happy about it!

When the schoolyear was over, I had 6 weeks off before I had to start my job.

I had to sign a contract that I would work there for three years, while I was going to high school, because that was the law!

I started my new job on the 1st of September of 1957, and I worked every day of the week except for one day when I had to go to high school. This job was three houses away from where my father lived, so now I saw him a little more. Sometimes he would tell me to come for lunch to his house. I did, but not very often, I felt I didn't belong there and was very uncomfortable. Besides I did not want to get in trouble, if my stepfather would have found out.

My father had two children with his second wife. A girl who was born in 1949 her name is Christa and a boy born two years later named Bernhard. I didn't get to know them well until much later in my life. Renate and Hans were much closer to them because they spend more time in their house.

Back to my job, I was able to go home for lunch because the store closed for two hours every day. I did not like my lady boss; she was very mean and always made me feel stupid and she told me I should consider myself lucky that she hired me

In her store, we sold all kinds of appliances, lighting fixtures, plugs and everything else that had to do with electricity. We also took in small items to fix and I had to learn all that, which didn't really interest me.

I felt I was back home helping my stepfather with his dumb hobbies on Sundays. I think my boss was so mean because she

INGRID DE MICHELE

was never able to have children. Her husband was a nice man and he realized soon that I was not happy working in the store with his wife. Most of the time he worked in the field installing electricity and he also handled all the books.

Chapter 23

MOST OF THE days I walked home for lunch. It was just the other end of the town. In the middle of the town was a large bank and many people hung out there for lunch. One day when I was right there in the middle, I had to cross the street and when I stepped of the curb my heel got caught in the cobblestone and I fell in front of all the people who hung out over there. I was so embarressed because my skirt flew over my head and you could see my underwear. No one helped me get up and when I finally did, I ran home with scrapped knees. It took me a long time to go that way again!

There was another girl working in the store with me and her name was Gerlinde. My boss liked her very much, probably because she came from a much better family than I. I had to work much harder than her. She was already in her last year of learning.

I was so miserable at my job in the first year, that I was trying to get out of my contract, but I couldn't.

My lady boss sent me sometimes to her house and do all her ironing which I was not supposed to do, and I told her husband. He told me to have patience and he would speak to his wife because he wanted to teach me some of the paperwork. She did not like the idea that I complained to her husband and told me so.

I was almost finished with my first year when I found out that she paid me the incorrect amount of salary which was set by the government. She only paid me 25 Deutsch mark which was about 6 dollars at that time, and I was supposed to be paid 50 Deutsch marks a month.

When I told her, she got mad at me, but I did not care, I was intitled to get the right amount and all the back pay.

I had only 5 marks a month for myself, everything else I had to give up at home. My stepfather expected me to buy clothes, books and my personal things I needed for 5 marks, which was impossible. I always fought with him about that, but he didn't care. He would tell me, because now that I was working, I would have to pay for the food I was eating at home.

I thought he was crazy!

There was a boy I knew from school and he invited me sometimes to go to the movies with him. When I asked at home if I could go, the answer was most of the time, no. When I finally could go it was on a Sunday afternoon and I had to come straight home. My stepfather knew exactly when the movie was over and how long it would take me to walk home. If I was only a few minutes late he would be waiting with the strap to hit me.

To this day I still have marks on my back when he used his strap!

Chapter 24

ONE DAY MY sister Helga came home for the weekend and she wanted to go out and meet some friends. She was sixteen years old and my stepfather would not let her go. That Saturday night my mother and him had plans to go visit someone so they wanted Helga to watch us.

When they left, they always locked the door behind them so we couldn't leave.

There was a small attic window in the apartment which led out to the roof and from there you could climb into the hallway outside from our apartment.

Well, Helga decided she was not going to stay home, so she told us she would climb out that window and go out and promised to be home before my mother and her husband. With that, she started to climb out the window and Freddy and I were so afraid and scared for her and for us, because we knew if she won't be home on time, we all would be in trouble.

Whenever one of us would do something wrong, we would never tell on them, even if it meant we were all punished, that has been like that since we been small. That night the time passed slowly and with every little noise we heard outside we thought they be coming back, and Helga was not home yet. Thank god she got home about ten minutes before them, she quickly got undressed and went to bed. We all made believe we were sleeping when they walked in.

Later we would tell my mother and she did not tell on us. She was just not strong enough to go against him.

Sometimes she did and then he was horrible towards her. My mom was working already for a while in a cafeteria with soldiers. It was hard work and she would be very tired when she got home, but my mother never complained, because of her job, there was a little more money in the house and therefore our meals were better.

Helga had hated her job as much as I did but she was able to get out of it because she was able to proof that they overworked her. She got a new job in Munich which was 35 kilometers from Erding. She was so much happier there and only came home once a month.

The second year on my job got somewhat better. I could help Herr Scheichl with his paperwork, which took me out of the store. I was now making 75 Deutsch marks a month and I had to give 50 marks to my mother. At least I had a little more money for myself.

I did not like working in the store, so I only did what I was told. One day my boss told me to climb on a ladder to rearrange some lighting fixtures. I had to disconnect and reconnect the wires and she forgot to shut of the electricity to the lights and I got a shock of 220 volt which knocked me right of the ladder.

I was shaking for some time and it scared her to death. When it was over, she never even asked me how I felt and that got me so mad that I told her husband, when he came in. He was furious with her, because he told her many times, that was not our job, he had electricians for that.

Gerlinde the other girl who was working in the store with me was not very nice to me. Many times, she told me that she would never associate with me because she came from a better family.

One day I saw her taking money from merchandise we sold and put it in her pocket, which really belonged to my boss. When I questioned her about it, she would tell me not to say anything and she give me some of the money. She also told me if I would say something, she would say it was me and who do I think our boss would believe, not me because she liked her very much.

She treated her like a daughter. I knew it was wrong, but I was too shy and nervous to say anything. Little that we knew my boss suspected that money was missing, and she confronted Gerlinde and just as she told me she would, she told her that it was me. She believed her and I couldn't proof it otherwise.

When I was alone again with her husband, I told him what she did and her husband believed me and he told me if there was any more trouble with Gerlinde, I should come to him. I was so glad that he believed me!

INGRID DE MICHELE

Chapter 25

IN 1957 MY sister Renate and her boyfriend Mike became proud parents of a baby boy and they named him Joseph, he was so cute. They moved into a small apartment in Langengeisling a few miles from my hometown. Mike still wanted to marry Renate, but his Sargent still would not allow it.

My brother Hans left the farm where he was working and got a job on the base where all the soldiers were stationed. I think it was my father who finally helped him get the job because he was also working on the base. Hans did not move back home, instead he slept on the couch in Renate's apartment which was close to his job, until he was drafted in the army and then he was stationed in Landshut, which was a little further away.

Since Renate and Mike are together, they visited my father frequently and sometimes asked me to come along. This is how I got to know my father and his wife a little better.

In January of 1958 Mike was transferred to France and they moved there with baby Joseph.

At the same time Helga was finished with high school and Renate asked her if she wanted to move to France with her. Helga was happy about that because she did not want to move back home, but my mom got upset.

Chapter 26

HELGA TOLD HER, it would be much better for her, she would get a job and help Renate with the coming baby. I would miss her a lot, but I knew in my heart it is the best for her.

In the summer of 1958, I had one-month vacation and Renate and Mike were visiting from France. She asked me if I wanted to go back with them to stay awhile, I would be able to take the train back. So, I did and was happy to see Helga again.

When I saw her, I knew that she wasn't too happy there.

She told me that she had met someone, and Renate did not like him, she always gave her trouble when she wanted to go out with him. Helga told me she loved him, and he is very good to her. As soon as Renate and Mike were going to the United states she would stay in France and marry her boyfriend.

When my vacation was over, I went back home on the train and back to the job I hated.

When Mike told his Sargent that Renate was expecting another child, he finally gave him permission to marry her. In March of 1959, Renate and Mike finally got married and they drove to Basel Switzerland to do just that.

In February of 1959,I turned 16 years old and because I never had a birthday party in my life, I asked my mother if she could make arrangements to go somewhere with her husband, so I could plan a little party for me and some friends. She said she would try, and she did one Saturday after my birthday. It was carnival time and that was good because they would stay out later.

I planned my party, went out and bought different color light-bulbs, I made some punch and had some Snacks. I invited some of my girlfriends, also my brother Freddy. Hans brought some of his friends with him that I knew. One of them had a little crush on me and he always said, he will marry me one day, which made me laugh.

I had a great time and we cleaned everything up before my mom came home. My stepfather never found out about it and I was grateful to my mom for letting me have this day!

Whenever it was possible, I tried to do something special for my mom, especially on Mother's Day!

As long as I could remember we all made Mother's Day special

INGRID DE MICHELE

for her. Even when we were small and had no money to buy her anything, we would get up very early in the morning and go across the street, where there was a beautiful evergreen and lilac bush.

We took lots of branches and with the evergreen we made a border around the table on a white tablecloth and put a vase with the lilacs in the middle. I loved lilacs, they smelled so good. We had handmade gifts when we were younger, and I always resided a poem. Every time I started reading the poem and it came to the word mother, I would start crying and couldn't continue and we all cried, this made my mom always smile and she had to fight back tears too!

My mom meant everything to me, and I always tried to be good and never give her any trouble. When I was working the two of us would sometimes go to the movies or for ice cream which we both loved very much, but never had any at home.

Chapter 27

MIKE WAS COMING to the end of his 5th year in the air force and he decided to take his family to the United states. Renate was very excited and before they left, they all came to say goodbye. She told us that Helga would be back soon, but I knew better!

Helga was already expecting a child from her boyfriend and right after Renate left to go to America, Helga married her boyfriend Alfred and made her life in France. His parents loved her, and she was very happy. We were all sorry that we couldn't see her get married and celebrated with them at the small party her in-laws gave them.

In the meanwhile, my brother Hans was still stationed in Landshut and he came home very seldom. I had more contact with my father then and one day my father asked me if I wanted to go with him to visit Hans. I had not seen him for a while, and I was happy to go. My father and I took off on his motorcycle to see him. It started to rain a little that day, but I did not care, we had a good time and Hans was happy to see us.

Hans told us that he met a girl and he liked her very much, but her parents were strict and would not allow her to stay out late, but he could come to her house.

When my brother Hans was in school, he had a hard time learning and there was no one to help him because my mother was working a lot and my stepfather couldn't care less. So, he was always behind especially in reading. He had told his girlfriend, but she did not care and said she would help him.

It became very serious with them Hans wanted to marry her. Her name was Rosemarie and she was still in high school and learning how to become a seamstress at her aunts' business.

Her parents did not want her to be married yet and they did not like that Hans was not catholic. He told them that he would be happy to change and go for instructions for her, but they wanted them to wait until she finished her education.

They waited and he started to go for religious instructions and that pleased her parents, it showed them that he was sincere about their daughter.

Chapter 28

I WAS NOW sixteen years old and I wanted to go out for New Year's Eve. I had met a boy I liked, and he invited me to a dance. I had saved to buy me a new dress, but again my stepfather said I couldn't go. He was working at a gas station that day and before he came home, I got dressed and went out anyway. My mother was very nervous because she knew what would happen when I got home, but I did not care.

Well, when I got home about 1 am he was waiting for me with the strap and immediately started beating me with it and he tore my brand-new dress right of me. I became so outraged and screamed at him," if you don't stop hitting me, I will go to the police and have you arrested for all the things you did to me in my life". Even my mother tried to stop him, and I was afraid he was going to hit her when she told him from now on, he could not interfere anymore, and I only had to answer to her.

She told him, Ingrid never gave us any problem and was always a good girl. He did not like what he was hearing and kept on screaming so loud that the neighbors came to the door. They all hated him!

I think he was so mad because he knew he could not control me ever again. I was so happy that my mother finally stood on my side, even though she knew she had to suffer for it. I told him also he better starts treating my mom like a wife and not a slave. I don't know where I got the courage to say all that, but I also knew that I would be moving out after I graduate in July and my mother knew it too. I would look for a job away from my hometown even if it hurt my mother, but she understood.

The boy who took me dancing that night was furious when he found out what my stepfather had done, and he saw the strap marks on me. He wanted to go to my house and beat him up, but I did not want him to get in trouble.

I always thought how nice it would be when someone loves you, but not like a mother and I thought my boyfriend really did. He treated me nice and always wanted to do things for me. He even spoke of getting married one day when we were older. He was two years older than me and already had a good job. I was very naive and believed everything he said.

We were going out for some time already and when we had the weekend of, we went many times to the town park. One day we were in the park and he started kissing me. I was getting nervous because I thought I could get pregnant if I let him tongue kiss me, but he said that was silly.

We laid down in the grass and he started touching me in places I did not like. He kept telling me when you in love that is what you do, and he told me that he wanted to make love to me. I did not know what he meant, and he said just do what I tell you and I was stupid enough not to stop him.

INGRID DE MICHELE

Chapter 29

$\sim\!\!\sim$

IT TOOK ALL about five minutes and the whole thing was over. I started to cry and wanted to go home immediately. When I got home, I saw that there was blood on my underwear and that made me more nervous. Thank god my mother and her husband were not at home!

I heated up some water and put it in a basin and with a cloth and lots of soap, I locked myself in the bathroom and scrubbed myself thoroughly.

When my mother came home, she realized that something happened and asked me if I was okay, I said yes and confided in her later.

I knew she wouldn't tell my stepfather. She said she was sorry that she never spoke to me about such things and hoped that he didn't make me pregnant. I prayed a lot in that time and swore to myself that if I was not pregnant, I will never let any man do that to me again until I was ready.

Well, god listen to me and I got my period two weeks later, I was so grateful. This boy who said he loved me so much, naturally only wanted one thing from me and then moved on to the next girl.

He made me so mad, that every time I saw his red shiny moped that he adored, I took some things off.

Even my girlfriend helped me when I told her what happened. I knew exactly where he would park it when he was at work, so I had easy access to it. He asked me once if I knew anything about it, but I made believe I did not know what he was talking about. I knew it was wrong, but I didn't care.

Months after my old boyfriend broke up with me, a friend introduced me to someone new. I was not interested to go out. with anyone but I liked him. He was very respectful to me and after we saw each other a few times, he said he wanted me to meet his parents. They were nice people and said they like me as their son's girlfriend.

One day when I was at their house, they kept asking me questions about my religion. I had told them that I was raised Lutheran until my stepfather made us join this other religion.

They informed me that this was not a recognized religion and they told me if I ever considered going back to become Lutheran again, they would speak to the priest for me. I don't know why it was so important to them, but I wanted to get out of that other religion and told them so.

INGRID DE MICHELE

I went to the priest with them and he arranged for me to convert back. My boyfriend's parents were pleased but when my stepfather found out he was livid, but he had nothing to say and my mom only said it was my choice if that is what I wanted.

Not long after that my boyfriend decided, because I was going to move away for a new job in the summer, he was too young to be so involved, so we agreed to go our separate ways.

I never had any problems to make friends and when I met a boy who was interested in me, I always told them that I just wanted to be friends. There were lots of soldiers in Erding who had girlfriends back home and all they wanted was someone to go to the movies or dancing with and that was okay with me.

Chapter 30

I GRADUATED IN July of 1960, and I had many offers to work in different cities, but I accepted a job in Munich, because I did not want to be that far away from my mother.

I was hired as a salesgirl in a large supermarket called Tengelmann. I was to start on the first of September. The company offered to pay a part of the rent and I roomed with a girl who worked for the same company.

I decided to take the summer off and visit Helga and Alfred in France. She just had a baby girl and had a rough time. She had gotten a bad infection on her breasts and was in a lot of pain. I was glad to help her, but I felt sorry for her that she was already a wife and a mother because she did not have a life of her own yet.

I swore to myself that I will make sure, not be making the same mistake and be married that young. I always dreamed of meeting my night and shining armor and have a fairytale wedding and then start a family!

So far none of my siblings had that!

I started my new job in September and even though it was hard work because my boss made me in charge of the vegetable department and I had to carry heavy crates, but I was happy to be there.

The room I shared with the girl had also moved away from her family and her name was Loni. She was older than me, but we got along great. I missed my mom and after I received my first paycheck which was only once a month, I tried to go home every weekend to see her. Whenever I came home, my stepfather wanted money from me, because I was eating his food. He was a miserable man and I couldn't believe he expected me to pay for my dinner.

I did notice that every time one of us, who were not his children moved out, he became a little nicer to my mom. My stepbrother was now 14 years old and started to work as a mechanic. He knew how bad his father was to us, but what could he do?

Whenever I came home for the weekend, Freddy wanted me to take him to the park-cafe. There you were able to sit outside if the weather was good and do some dancing, which I loved.

I was always able to get dancing partners and one weekend there was this guy, who was the son of parents who owned a very large farm nearby. Nobody wanted to dance with him when he asked the girls, because he was not very good looking and he always had a farm odor on him.

There is a time when a girl could ask the guy to dance and they called it Damen Wahl and I felt bad for him because no one ask him, so I asked him to dance. He looked so happy and it turned out that he was a fabulous dancer and we became good friends.

I saw him every time I came home and went to the park-cafe.

He wanted to become more then friends, but I told him that is all that I want. I did not feel any more for him and I didn't want to lead him on.

I told him if I don't have anyone else, I would go dancing with him. He always said to me, that I was afraid to love him because I didn't want to live on a farm, and he assured me, he would build me a nice house and that I would not have to help him on the farm.

I wished sometimes that I could love him because he deserved to be loved by someone. I was friends with him for a long time and was so sad when I found out many years later that he died in a car crash and was never married!

INGRID DE MICHELE

Chapter 31

I WAS NOW already working three months in Munich and I loved being on my own. The only bad thing was, there was no trolley connection to my job, and I had to walk to work and, in the winter, it was very cold, and it was a long way. At least now I had a warm coat and boots.

My stepfather started giving me orders every time I came home, and I told my mom that I was not coming home so much anymore.

I became very close with my roommate Loni and she invited me to come to her parents' house. We took a train to Wuerzburg which is another region of Germany and her family made me feel very welcome. She had another sister who just got married and a younger brother. We went there several times and each time, we had lots of fun, she showed me all around town!

When we had no plans for the weekend, we went out dancing

on Saturday night. There was a big dance hall, not close to our apartment but we were able to take the trolley car. We always had fun there, but we never stayed out too late!

When I came home for Christmas holiday my mother told me that she received a letter from Renate. She told her how much she liked living in America and that Mike is starting a job at Pan American airways soon and if everything goes well, they will come and visit next summer.

We had two and a half days off for the holiday, but I only stayed at home for Christmas eve and took the train back to spend the rest of the holidays with Loni and our landlords.

The months flew by and the weather was getting warmer and soon it was the beginning of summer.

Our landlords drove many times to a lake when the weather was hot, and they offered to take us with them one day.

So, one Sunday in the beginning of summer, it was a beautiful day, we finally went to the lake. We packed some things to eat and drink and our landlords said they would take blankets.

When we got there, we went into the lake right of way. I was swimming with Loni and I told her lets swim across to the other side. I considered myself a good swimmer, because when I was in school, I took every swimming competition for rescues and received certificates for it.

Well, that day Loni was not in the mood to swim more; she wanted to lay out in the sun, so I decided to do it on my own.

My landlord and his wife and Loni were relaxing on the blankets. I started to swim and was about three quarters across when I developed a cramp in my leg, and it hurt bad and couldn't continue.

Chapter 32

I WAS WAVING to the shore for someone to see me, but they were only waving back. I had a hard time staying above the water and kept going up and down because the pain was so bad. Thank god, out of nowhere a small boat came along, they saw I was in trouble and pulled me out of the water. I was so exhausted and just lay in the boat for a while, before the two young men took me back to the shore. I couldn't thank them enough and I don't know what would have happened if they didn't come along. Loni and my landlords felt so bad, that they did not pay attention, but were happy I was safe. I never had any desire to swim that far out again.

A few weeks later, Renate and her family arrived from America. it was nice seeing them again and she had a lot to tell us about her new life in the united states. She stayed at my father's house and we made plans for all of us to get together the next weekend.

She contacted Helga in France and she said she would come too. I came home the following Saturday and some of my friends wanted me to go out with them so I could meet a soldier who was a buddy of one's boyfriend.

We all met at the ice cream parlor. It was a warm night and that is where I saw Herbert for the first time. I thought he was very handsome and very friendly. We seemed to hit it off right from the start and he asked me to go out with him again the next weekend and I agreed. I told him that I lived in Munich and that I would come down with the train and he said he would pick me up.

The next day we all met at my father's house to see Renate and Mike. Their boy Joseph was already 4 years old and her daughter Cathy was two, they were so cute. Renate told us of all the different and great things there are in America and Mike told me about his brother Jack. He said he is a real lady's man, always went out and driving his parents crazy. Renate was very happy that Mike had gotten the job at Pan American airways because it enabled them to come and visit more often.

Hans came down from Landshut with his fiancée Rosemarie and he told us he was getting married in December. We were also glad to see Helga and her little daughter Dominique. It was amazing for all of us to be together for the first time in my father's house and that he said it made him very happy. I thought his wife was very nice and she made us feel very comfortable. It was a chance for me to get to know her and her children better.

I had to leave that night to go back to Munich, but I was looking forward to seeing Herbert the following weekend.

My relationship with Herbert grew very quickly and I knew for the first time that I was in love. I never felt like that before. He treated me so special like no one ever did and when we saw each other he would always have a little gift for me. I told him, "you don't have to do that", but he said, I like seeing you happy!

When I introduced him to my mother, she liked him immediately and even my stepfather did to, but he took advantage of him because he had a car.

Every weekend we would do something that he had planned, or we met with our friends to go out together. When I couldn't come home, he would write me letters and I loved getting them. He knew how to write beautiful letters!

We were seeing each other about two months when I started getting bad pains in my legs. Sometimes it was so painful that I had trouble walking. My doctor told me to stay off my legs as much as I could, which meant I couldn't go to work. He also advised me to change my job, because when I told him what I did, he said that lifting and carrying heavy crates of vegetables caused me to get varicose veins.

Herbert had to carry me back and forth to the car when I had to go to the doctor; I was not allowed to walk much. I stayed at my mother's house for some of the weeks, which did not make my stepfather happy.

Before I went back to work, I told my boss that I could not do that same job anymore, so he gave me a different position on the register where I was able to sit. I had to wear heavy support stockings for a long time, and they did not look nice and were not very comfortable.

Chapter 33

ᴍ

MY BROTHER HANS'S wedding was coming close and I couldn't wait to see them get married. All this time he went for religious instructions and they had a baby son who was almost six months old and they were still living in Rosemarie's parents' house.

Being I had to work every Saturday I told my boss in advance that I needed to take off for the day of their wedding, but he would only give me a half a day. My father said he would take me to the wedding, but I had to be there early enough.

Well, it was December 16th, 1961 and that day everything went wrong. While I was still at work, we heard there was a plane crash in the city of Munich, and it crashed into trolley car after it clipped a steeple of a church and they said all the people on the plane died.

It made me very nervous because I did not know exactly what part of the town it was. When I left work, I walked home in a hurry to make up some time.

When I got home, my landlady informed me that the plane crashed into the same trolley that comes to our house and which I needed to get to the train station. So now, I would have to find another way of getting there. I was getting very upset because I knew if I don't make it home on time for my father to take me to the wedding, I have no other way of getting there and I would not see my brother get married.

When I finally got to the station, I was happy to see the train still on the track and I ran to get on it. I felt so rushed that I paid no attention if it was the right train. As the train pulled away, I realized that I did not recognize anyone, because usually I always saw people from my hometown. The train was pulling out of the station already going about 25 miles an hour, when I was told, it was not going to Erding. All I could think of, you must get of this train, so I took my bag opened the door and jumped off.

Extra-Ausgabe 10

Münchner Merkur

DIE FLUGZEUGKATASTROPHE

US-Maschine zerschellt am Hackerberg - Tragfläche gegen Turm von St. Paul - Straßenbahn im Flammenmeer - Mehr als 50 Tote

DIE STÄTTE DES GRAUENS: Auf der Strecke Laim/Martin-Greif-Straße, an Hackerberg zerschellte eine amerikanische Transportmaschine der amerikanischen Luftwaffe. Der Brand des explodierenden Flugzeugs verwandelte den Platz in ein Flammenmeer. In dem nur wenige Sekunden dauernden Inferno fanden mehr als 50 Menschen den Tod.

Erste Tote identifiziert

Erste Verletztenliste

Extra-Ausgabe 10

Chapter 34

I LANDED ON a pile of rocks, covered with snow and I fell directly on them with my face. I started to bleed immediately, and I grabbed a handkerchief to stop it. As I was standing there holding my bleeding nose, I realized what a stupid thing I had done. I also saw that the buckle of my coat was ripped off and I thought, god was on my side, because I could have been killed if my coat would have been caught.

Not only that, if my boss would have giving me the whole day off, I could have been on that trolley where the plane crashed into, because it was around the same time, I needed to get to the train on time.

When I started to walk back to the station along the tracks to the platform, there were all the people I knew from my hometown. They couldn't believe when they found out what I had done. I was also informed that I did miss the train I needed to meet my father. I knew then, I would not make it to Hans and

Rosemarie's wedding, and I was very upset and started to cry, it would have been my first wedding and it was my brother's.

When I finally got home, everyone had left and there was no way for me to get there. I wished Herbert had been here, but he went to see his parents this weekend. Now I was at home with my face and nose hurting me. I took some medication and cleaned the wound as best I could, so it won't get infected.

I fell asleep on the couch and woke up when my mother walked in. When she heard what I had done she slapped me right across the face. I was so stunned and started crying. My mother never hit me before but then she took me in her arms and told me how dangerous it was for me to jump of a moving train.

I knew it myself and wished I hadn't done it, because by now I had a bad headache which lasted for days and it took a long time before my nose healed. My mother then told me all about the wedding, how nice it was, and everyone was wondering why I was not there.

When Herbert came back and saw me, he also got mad that I did such a foolish thing. I told him it was a split- second decision and it was over.

It was only a few more days until Christmas, and I was sure this would be a much better Christmas for me because I was happy that Herbert was in my life and spending it with me.

I had bought myself a new suit that I was going to wear for the wedding, so now I wore it for Christmas. I wanted to look pretty for Herbert because he told me, we will be doing something special.

On Christmas eve there was my mother, stepfather and my brother Freddy at home and we all had a nice dinner together, that my mother made with love for all of us. When we finished dinner, my mom lit all the candles on the Christmas tree, and we sang Christmas songs.

So far it was my best Christmas!

When we finished singing, Herbert took my hand and told me how much he loved me and then took two gold rings from his pocket and asked me if I wanted to marry him? Well, I was so surprised but happy. I could not believe that he wanted to get engaged so soon and I asked him why.

He told me, that he would have to go away in February to a flight school for 6 months and he wanted me to know, that I belonged to him.

I accepted the ring and he put it on my left ring finger. The custom in Germany is when a couple gets engaged, they wear the ring on the left hand and when they get married, they use the same ring and put it on the right hand. I was happy but also sad, knowing he would have to leave soon, and I won't be able to see him for all that time.

We planned to spend every weekend together until then and we were planning our future together. He explained to me why I could not even visit him while he is in flight school, it was going to be a difficult course and he was not allowed of base.

Chapter 35

‑‑‑ ∿ ‑‑‑

RIGHT AFTER CHRISTMAS I was writing a letter to my sister Renate and I had mentioned that I got engaged and that my Fiancé must go away for six months starting February.

She answered me quickly and I was surprised what she had to say. Renate and Mike invited me to come to America for the six months Herbert would be away. I was confused and did not know what to do. I talked it over with my mother and Herbert and they both thought it would be a great opportunity and I should take advantage of it. I wrote Renate that I would accept her offer.

So, I asked my company if I could take a leave of absence for that time, and then I went to the German consulate to process my visa.

I was very busy the next month, because my departure date was set for February 3rd.

I was nervous about flying for the first time, especially after that plane crash a few weeks before, were so many people got killed.

Getting my papers together for my visa was a lot of work, I even had to have a physical examination with their doctor to prove I was not pregnant.

My company declined my leave of absence, so I had to quit my job and give up my room I shared with Loni. She was sad to see me go, because we became like sisters, but she said she would do the same thing if she had the chance. I promised to stay in touch, and I knew she would not be too lonely because she also had a steady boyfriend, who wanted to marry her.

Herbert received a week off before his leave and he invited me to meet his parents and stay a few days before I flew to America. He lived close to the Frankfurt airport and he wanted to show me around, so I would see were we would be living when we get married. Renate sent me an open ticket, so I could leave anytime, all I had to do is call the airline and tell them when I was ready.

Well, the day finally came, and I had to say goodbye to my mother, and it was not easy. We both cried and I told her six months is not long and it will go by quickly and I will be back.

I took the train to Frankfurt where Herbert picked me up. We drove to his parents' house and they were very nice people and welcomed me like a daughter. We had three days together and Herbert took me all around town. He showed me where he grew up, also where he worked before, he went into the service and he was planning to go back, once he got out.

Frankfurt was a large city and very busy and I did not like that too much, coming from a smaller town. One day we took a cruise on the Rhein river where we stopped in small villages, which were known for their wines. It was just beautiful, and I did not want the time to end.

The last night we all sat in the living room and had some wine we bought and spoke of America. After a while his parents said goodnight and left us alone. I was getting very sad and did not want to leave, but I knew Herbert was also leaving on the weekend and that made it a little easier.

Since we been going out together, Herbert never made any advances toward me, but this night we knew something was going to happen. We were sitting in his room on his bed and kissed and hugged and he asked me if he could make love to me. I was scared but I loved him, so I said yes only if he used protection. He was very gentle and all I could think about afterwards, was about my first time I let a man touch me, how different it is when you love someone. He kissed me goodnight and went to the other room, I was not comfortable sleeping in the same bed with his parents in the house.

The next day, after we had breakfast together, I said goodbye to his parents and they told me to have a good time and they were happy that they met me, and their son found such a sweet girl.

Herbert drove me to the airport and we both cried when we

INGRID DE MICHELE

said goodbye. He told me he would write me every day, so I won't forget him, even if it is only a few lines and I know he meant it.

He stayed with me until I was called to board the plane and I kissed him one more time and left.

Chapter 36

IT WAS VERY cold outside and there was lots of snow and it took a long time for the plane to take off. I was very nervous, but once we were up in the air, I became excited. I had a window seat and there was so much to see. We flew through the clouds and over lots of water; it was just beautiful to watch. I could not understand how a big airplane like this one, could stay up in the sky?

It was a nine-hour flight to the Idlewild airport in New York. When we got close to New York the captain informed us that we would be delayed because the weather was bad, and it was snowing.

I was looking out the window the whole flight and when we flew over New York, I was amazed how big everything looked.

When I was a child my friend Caroline used to tell me about New York, how great it is and I always thought all the people who live there must be rich.

Chapter 37

I WAS THINKING about Caroline and I wished she would have kept in touch, maybe we could have seen each other now. I haven't heard from her for many years and I guess when someone is apart for a while, you soon forget that person.

I was hoping, Mike would find out that the plane is delayed and not knowing made me nervous, because we were already two hours late.

I could see myself stranded in this new big city and nobody would be there to meet me. Naturally that was not the case and Renate and Mike were waiting for me when I came through customs.

Even though I knew Renate was having another baby I was surprised to see her and that she only had three more months to go. On the way to their house they told me that Mike's family would be there to welcome me. It was Sunday and they always had dinner together

As we got closer to the house, I became more nervous, I did not know much English and wondered what they thought of me. I was always a shy person and not good in meeting new people. We arrived at the apartment building where they lived, and I was overwhelmed how big those buildings were and there were so many.

When I walked into Renate's apartment I was surprised of the warm and friendly welcome Mike's family gave me. They made me feel very comfortable. They had lots of questions which I couldn't answer or understood, and I had to ask Renate what they said.

Everybody was there, Mike's mother and father, both of his sisters with their husbands, only his younger brother Jack was missing. Mike told me he was on a date and he would come later.

Renate and Mike's children were running around, they were now 5- and 2-years old. They were the first grandchildren of Mike's parents and they adored them.

I was worried about meeting Mike's brother Jack, I guess it was because he is a single young guy and I wondered what he would think of a young girl from another country. I was very tired because of the long flight and the six- hour time difference got to me. Mike's mother had prepared dinner and she asked me if I liked spaghetti and meatballs. I did not know what meatballs were, but I knew I was not crazy over spaghetti, though I would have never told her that.

Mike's sister Rose was setting the table and just before we all sat down, Jack finally walked through the door, he was very handsome.! I was still sitting on the living room chair and he came over and kissed and hugged me and I felt myself blushing, I was so embarressed. I had never had anybody make so much fuss over me. There was not much kissing and hugging going on in my house!

Jack started to talk to me, but I did not understand one word, he was speaking so fast and Mike told him to slow down so I could understand. From that moment on, he would always speak slowly.

We all sat down to eat, and I felt his eyes on me and it made me very uncomfortable. The food was delicious even the spaghetti, it was different from what I was used to.

After dinner we had cake and coffee. On the cake was written "Ingrid welcome to America" which I never seen before, but it was very nice. It made me feel good that Mike's family did all that for me and I knew from the start that they were good people and I liked them very much. I had never seen so much love in a family! I was thinking of my mom and I missed her already, but I know she would have been happy for me!

I noticed Jack kept on looking at my legs and I was wondering why. I did find out later because I had very hairy legs. He was very funny and friendly, and I could tell we were going to get along and become friends. After we finished with coffee, Mike's family said goodbye, they lived in an area called Brooklyn which was another part of New York and where Renate lived was called Far Rockaway.

Mike told me that it would take them over an hour to get home because of the Sunday traffic, which puzzled me. I had no idea what he meant about traffic, in my hometown there were not many cars. Munich had more cars, but nobody ever spoke of traffic.

Once everyone was gone, I asked Renate to show me where I would sleep, I was very tired and had trouble keeping my eyes open. I slept in the kids' room that night and as tired as I was, I could not fall asleep; besides I was thinking of all the people I left behind.

The next day my life in America began and it was very different from Germany. Renate's kids kept me busy and always wanted to play with me. I was not used to having small kids around me and they were exhausting.

There was lots of snow outside, so we went downstairs and played in the snow building a snowman. At night Renate and Mike went out and I stayed home and watched the kids.

One week had past when I received my first letter from Herbert. He told me all about the new school and how much he had to learn, but he assured me he will always find time to write. After that I received a letter from him almost every day and that made me feel good because I already felt homesick.

Renate said to me that she thought he was crazy writing me every day, but I didn't think so because I missed him a lot. Time went by very slowly and I was beginning to get bored spending all my time at home with Renate's kids. I wanted to go to work but Renate wanted me to stay home. I had no time for myself and became miserable. I was getting the feeling that Renate only invited me to be their built-in babysitter, because she and Mike went out all the time.

They lived very close to a beach and when I had time I went there and looked across the ocean with tears in my eyes and wishing I was on the other side.

Sometimes Mike's brother Jack came over on Saturday nights to babysit with me and once the children were in bed, he would teach me English. I had learned to speak and understand already quite a lot. I always told Renate and Mike to only speak English with me and if I didn't understand I would ask them what they said. Jack became a good friend to me, and he was the only one I could tell how I felt.

Chapter 38

TWO WEEKS AFTER I arrived was my 19th birthday and Jack told Renate that he wants to take me to the movie's. I was so excited all day and waited for Jack to pick me up. It was the first time I went out somewhere without the kids hanging on me. We took a train to New York city and had to change trains several times before we got there.

Jack tried very hard to explain everything to me, so I could understand, but I always had to tell him to speak slowly. I had made a big mistake and wore high heel shoes that day, I did not realize how much we had to walk. My shoes made a squeaking sound and Jack thought it was funny, but I was embarressed.

Once we arrived at the movie theater Jack kept on asking me if I wanted something. I just always said no, I didn't want him to spend so much money on me. I knew he was not earning a lot of money and besides I was just happy to be out of the house. I didn't understand a lot of the movie, it was a religious film called the king of kings, but I had a great time and I thanked him many times for taking me there.

He asked me if it was okay with me , if he comes over when Renate and Mike go out and they did almost every Saturday. I told him I would like that because Jack and I got to know each other well. He would tell me about his girl and me him about Herbert. So, every Saturday he came to babysit with me, because his girlfriend never went out with him on that day, she was Jewish, and he told me that they don't go out on Saturday's. I was glad that he would want to come over, so at least I had someone to talk to besides kids.

I told him that I was not happy because I was not working and earning some money and I was always home. He said to me if you really want to work go and find a job where you don't have to speak so much. I decided that I would, and told Renate the next day, she was not happy about it, but I did not care.

I had been on my own for almost two years and I liked being independent. So, the next day I took the bus into the next town and I planned to go from store to store until I had a job.

The first store I went to was called Woolworth and they hired me as a cashier and helping on the floor filling up merchandise. I was offered $2.50 an hour and I was very happy, and I told them I could start anytime.

When I got home, I told Renate the good news, but she didn't care. So, I started working the following Monday. I was so excited about my first job in America and when I told Jack about it he was glad for me, the job though did not turn out so great because when I was offered the position the boss told me that I would be mainly on the register because I could handle the American money.

It was mostly though the other way around and he made me do lots of cleaning. Once I overheard him telling someone," give Ingrid all these jobs because the German people are known to be very clean", that made me mad, but I was too shy to say anything and I did not want to lose the job.

I did not mention it to Renate, because I knew what she would say, so I stuck it out. I was there about a month when I was told to rearrange glass cubicles on a counter, when suddenly, a glass shattered into thousand pieces, while I was bending over and broken pieces of glass got into my eyes. I got so scared and screamed until my boss came over to see what happened.

He saw that I couldn't open my eyes and realized he needed to take me to a doctor or hospital. There was an eye doctor across the street and when he took me there the doctor told him to take me to the hospital, which he did. They notified Renate by phone but there was no way for her to get me and my boss told her he would drive me home once they release me.

They worked on my eyes for some time and the doctor told me that I was lucky it didn't cut my eye, only scratched it badly.

He put patches on both eyes, and I was told that I needed to wear them for at least one week. I was given drops which I had to put in twice a day and then put the patch back on.

He said that my right eye was more scratched, and I may have to keep the patch on longer. My boss was very nervous the whole time and he was concerned what I would do. He kept telling me I should not worry about anything and that he will pay for the doctor and hospital. I was glad to hear that because I was not insured in the united states.

When he drove me home and brought me to the door, Renate became very upset to hear what happened and when my boss was gone she said" I told you not to go to work, now I have to take care of you and I only have one more month before the baby is born". I was so mad that this accident happened because it meant again, I had to stay in the house, and I needed Renate's help.

I even had to ask her to read Herbert's letters to me and answer one, so he knew I couldn't write him for a while. He let me know that he was very worried about me and wished me speedy recovery.

Also, when Jack found out, he came over the next day to see how I was doing. He also offered to take me back to the doctor when I needed to go again. I had lots of pain in my eyes and I was so mad that this happened.

I did not let my mother know; I didn't want to worry her. I knew it would be hard for Jack to take me to the doctor because he did not live close by and had to take a few trains to get there.

Renate told Jack though, that Mike would take me. The first

week was very hard and I was glad when the doctor took off the left patch. I had to keep the right patch on for three more weeks and my eyes were irritated for a long time.

I did not go back to work at Woolworth when I was better. Renate gave birth to a baby girl the beginning of May and she needed my help.

I knew though as soon as she would be back on her feet, I would look for another job. I did not want to stay home, and I told Renate and Mike that.

It was not easy finding a job and I was getting more homesick. I still went to the beach at night and cried; I was so unhappy!

Every day, I was anxious for the mail to arrive, to get Herbert's letters. I received one almost every day. I was not happy here and I had no one to talk to, except for Mike's brother, whenever he came over to keep me company. I would tell him how lonely I was.

I did not like living by Renate and Mike because I was so restricted. I know they paid for my ticket and maybe they meant well, but I thought I would have more freedom.

It was important for me to find a job as soon as possible because I decided that I would go back to Germany, when I had enough money for a ticket.

It was not easy to find a job and I was getting frustrated. I was reading the want ads for a long time until I finally saw something that caught my eye. It read that they were looking for young foreign people to sell magazines, you had to be willing to travel and they offered full insurance and good pay.

When I told Renate, she didn't think it was a good idea, but I had to do something, so I called Jack and told him that I was thinking about this job.

He also thought that is was no good. He felt it was a scam, but he offered to take me there if they wanted to interview me.

I was so happy when I heard they wanted to meet me and gave me a time and day. Jack drove me to New York city; it was in the so-ho district and the building was a huge high rise. I had never been in a tall building like that and I thought these people had to be rich. Jack waited downstairs for me, and I was nervous when I went up and rang the bell.

A man of about 35 to 40 years answered the door and I told him who I was.

He invited me in, and we walked to the living room and he told me to sit. I was so impressed with what I saw, the apartment was huge, and I was wondering what my mother would think if she saw this place. She probably thinks this apartment is as big as a castle and there would be room for 5 families to live here, rather than one.

He asked me if I wanted to see the rest of this place, I guess he knew how amazed I was, you could see all of Manhattan from the big windows. After he showed me around, we sat again, and he explained to me what the job was about. He told me, I would be working with another person for the first two weeks until I learned it and then be on my own.

I would be away for a month, then come back for a week before we would go to another city. It sounded all good to me and I accepted the position.

He told me when we were going to leave and what I had to do to get ready. When I got back downstairs to where Jack was waiting, I told him that I took the job, but he was not happy when I told him that I always had to go to different places.

I told him I can take care of myself and I had to get away and if the job would not work out, I could always come back.

Well, we drove home and I told Renate and Mike, (Renate informed me that she wanted to be called Rene from now on) and they seemed upset that I was planning to leave.

I had to get my things together what I needed. My new boss was going to pick me up on Saturday and when the day came, I said goodbye to everyone and I told Rene and Mike that I hoped they would understand that I had to be more independent, but they were not happy.

Chapter 39

━━━━◆◆◆━━━━

My boss came with a big Cadillac and I felt special to drive in it. Before I left, I spoke to Jack to say goodbye and he told me, if I had any problems and the job would not work out to call him and he would get me.

We drove to a town called Rochester, NY and checked into a hotel. I met more people who were coming from different places. Some girls and boys were already working in the area and I was introduced to one girl who I was going to share the same room with. She was a few years older than me and very pretty, she was working for the company for a while. She was assigned to me, to teach me the job. She told me how much she liked it and showed me her bank book how much she was able to save.

What came to my mind was how fast can I save my money so I could go back to Germany. The following day we all had to meet in my bosses' room, and he gave all the new people some papers that he wanted us to read and memorize. He advised us that we had one day to study and then we would be going out with our assigned person.

There was a boy Kurt who started the same day as me and he was the same age and from Germany. He was very nice, and I liked him immediately. We took the papers and each of us went to our room to learn. When I started to read, I could not believe what I was reading. They wanted us to tell the people that we were students from east Germany and that we escaped over the wall and had to leave our family behind, and we were trying to save money to go to college in this country.

The reason for these lies was so the people would feel sorry for us and buy more magazines, which we offered to sell. Well, I had a hard time excepting these lies, but I thought of the money I could make and what I wanted to do with it. If I was not going along with this, I would have to go back to my sister's house and start all over again to find a job.

I made up my mind that I was trying to do my best to do this and the next day I went out with the girl who I was supposed to learn from. Our boss drove us to this rich section of Rochester, and we were going from house to house to sell the magazines and telling our lies.

The whole week I went out with her and I was not looking forward to be doing this on my own the following week.

Several times during the week when we got back to the hotel, she would ask me if I could hang out in the lobby for about an hour because she would have a male friend coming and she

INGRID DE MICHELE

wanted to be alone. I didn't want her to be mad at me even though I was tired from walking around all day, but I said okay and went downstairs. I was surprised she had so many male friends in a town where she was not very long.

The next week I went out on my own! I was going from house to house and saying those lies. Lots of people felt sorry for me and bought many magazines.

One day, it was already late I rang the bell on this beautiful house and a very nice lady opened the door. I told her my story and she felt so sorry for me, she invited me in. I met her husband and he was also a nice man.

They told me about their only daughter, who was away at school and how lonely they are without her. They wanted to know more about my life, and I felt bad making up more lies. I could see how much they felt sorry for me and that made me feel terrible. I thought to myself," I don't think I can do this much longer."

The couple invited me to come back on the weekend, so we could talk some more, and she wanted to cook dinner for me. I wasn't sure if this was such a good idea, but I was lonely, so I said I would try.

That night when I got to the hotel late and went up to my room, I walked in and was shocked to see my roommate having sex with a much older man. She acted like I shouldn't be there and told me to wait downstairs until she came to get me.

I was so upset and mad and I could not understand what she was doing. When she finally came down with the man, he walked out and I went upstairs to the room.

When she came back I told her I did not like what was going on and she told me "don't be so naïve, how do you think I made all this money I saved, don't be stupid, you could do the same thing" and that this job we had was not that great.

From that moment on I knew I was not going to stay there, and I had to figure out how to get home. The next day that young boy named Kurt who started the same time with me, told me that he was not happy either and he wanted to go home too.

I was already twice invited by those nice people I met and when I finally went, they offered to take me in to their house to live and they would help me go back to school. They said that they spoke to their daughter and she was happy they met me. I was so shocked and ashamed, that I wanted to tell them right there, that everything is a lie but at that moment I did not know how to make it right.

The next weekend Kurt and I and a few others went to a dance club, there was a contest going on we were all unhappy with our job, but we needed a little fun and we were making plans how to get away. I had called Jack during the week and told him what was going on and he told me that he will try to come to Rochester which he did on Saturday. He came with us to the dance club and we had lots of fun and Kurt and I even won the twisting contest.

Jack had to go back home, and we told him, if we couldn't convince our boss to take us home for the next weekend, we would hitchhike back to New York. The following day I woke up with an excruciating toothache and I couldn't go to work. My boss took me to the dentist, and I was shocked when he told me that I had four cavities in my front teeth and the he said it probably was from the change of food.

When I was living in Germany, my diet was totally different and I never ate vegetables from a can, always fresh and he thought that was the reason for the cavities. I spend most of that week at the dentist office, so I did not get a chance to see those nice people who offered to help me.

Kurt and I decided we were not staying any longer and each of us made up a story why we needed to go home.

We knew our boss was going back to New York the following Saturday and we asked him to take us along. He said he would and will pick us up again on Monday to take us back, but we had no intentions of doing that. That Friday before I left, I went to those nice people and told them both the truth.

They were very surprised to hear what I had to say, but also happy I would get back to my family. I told them that I was going to save enough money to go back to Germany to be with my fiancé. I also told them how ashamed I was, but they said they understood why I did it.

When I left on Saturday and arrived in New York, our boss dropped us of at the train station.

We had not much with us because we couldn't let him know we were not coming back. I wished Kurt all the best and he told me that he also wants to go back to Germany soon. I first called Jack to let him know that I was in New York and then I called Rene to let her know I was coming back.

When I got home, I told Rene and Mike what was going on that job and Mike was mad.

He called my boss and told him that I was not coming back and that he should make arrangements to get all my things delivered to me.

Needless to say my boss was very upset and he told my brother-in law that it was not his responsibility, but Mike made him understand, if he was not going to do it , he will report him to the right authorities about his business.

Within one week I had all my belongings and I was glad this chapter of my life was over. I realized then I should have listened to Jack!

When I got home there were lots of letters from Herbert waiting for me and I was so excited. He told me how much he missed me and that he still had a lot to learn and he may have to stay longer than 6 months. I told Rene what he said, and she said well, then you can stay with us until he finishes school, but that did not make me happy. I answered him and told him what has been going on and of my plans to save money so I could come back and how homesick I was.

INGRID DE MICHELE

Chapter 40

It was already the end of June and again I had no work, so my priority was to find another job quickly. I had learned a lot these last few weeks and my English improved, which gave me more confidence about looking for work. Throughout all this, I always kept in touch with my mother and I was glad to hear she was doing okay. I think she was happy because she had a much better job and that gave her a better life.

I read the want ads every day and went on several interviews until I was hired as a cashier in a clothing store, who specialized in larger women's sizes.

I was so glad to be working and making money. The job was not close to where I lived, and I had to take a train to get there.

Most of the ladies who worked at this store were middle aged and elderly. I was hoping for some young people, so I could make some friends. One lady was very nice to me and she sort of took me under her wings. She was from a Greek heritage and it always amazed me, how many people in America came from all over the world, which I found fascinating.

Where I grew up in Germany, I only knew German people, except for the soldiers who were stationed there and most of them were Americans!

At my new job there was an elderly lady working, she was the aunt of the famous singer Neil Diamond and I heard that she was of Jewish Heritage and she made me know that she hated me because I was German.

I found out later that she was in a concentration camp when she was young and she was treated very badly, she still had her number on her arm and that is why she had so much hatred for me. She tried all kinds of things to get me fired but my friend knew what she was doing and always stood by me.

One day I overheard her saying to someone that she will hurt me, like my people did to her but my boss found out and spoke to her. Later I had a chance to talk to her and I told her how sorry I was, but that I could not help what happened to her, that I was only a baby when all that was going on and that most German people were upset and very sorry what Hitler did to the Jewish people.

I said to her, I could also have hatred against the American people, because they bombed my hometown. After that talk it got a little better to work with her and soon after she retired.

Sometime in July, I was not getting many letters from Herbert and that made me sad because it was the only thing that kept me going. I was hoping that nothing was wrong.

My sister kept telling me that she thought my fiancé was probably having a good time without me, but I did not like hearing that and it made me mad that she would even say that.

When I finally received a letter from him again, he said he wanted to break our engagement. He believed that he was not ready to get married and he didn't want to tie me down. He even asked for the ring back!

I was so devastated and walked to the beach and cried and cried and I was so sorry that I even came to this country. I used to be such a happy person and since I came to America nothing was like I thought it would be.

I had no one to talk to, who would understand, my sister certainly didn't. I used to talk to Jack about Herbert, and he was a good listener and I could not wait to see him on the weekend.

I wrote a letter to Herbert to ask him why he would want to break up, that we do not have to get married yet, we could wait until he was ready, and we should have more time to get to know each other anyway. When he wrote back, he did not explain why he wanted to break our engagement, but just said "this is what I want" and I should send his ring back.

When I went to work the next day, my lady friend, who was like a mother to me, knew right of way that something happened to me, I felt so sad!

She did not ask me but waited for me to tell her. she told me how sorry she was but said the pain will pass and maybe it will be for the best!

Many times, I thought that I shouldn't have gotten engaged so soon because we really did not know each other that well. I think I was at that time just happy to have someone, who said they loved me, and he would take me away from the life I had!

When I saw Jack that weekend, he took me for a ride, so we could talk alone. He understood and tried to comfort me. He told me "now you don't have to go back to Germany so soon, and you can stay a little longer". I told him that I didn't think so, I wanted to be on my own again and I did not see that happening if I stayed.

I said I will work until I have enough money saved for my return ticket and some to keep me going until I found a new job and apartment. I knew I was not going back to my mom's house, but I was sure I could get my old job back; they were always looking for people.

When I saw Jack the next time, he told me that he broke off with his girlfriend, I asked him why and he told me, he was never serious about her and his family did not like that she was not a Christian girl.

Now, he had more time and he came over more often to keep me company when I had to babysit. He continued to teach me more English and when he got paid, he invited me to go to the movies. I was still very upset over my break-up with Herbert, but I did not always talk about it with Jack because he tried very hard to make me feel better. He became such a good friend!

Sometimes we would meet his friends at a fast food place in Brooklyn and we always had lots of fun because they were all young people.

Jack was very popular and funny, and everyone wanted to hang out with him!

Almost every Sunday we would go to Jack's family in Brooklyn for dinner. I loved going there because I never had such closeness in my family. I got to love Jack's mom and dad, they were great people, especially his father, he was a loving man and many times I wished he was my father, I would have had a much better life.

Every time we were there, they always spoke of what they did when they were young. There was always lots of laughter in the house. They never had a lot of money but much love. Both Jack's sisters were married but they had no children yet. His older sister Rose had been pregnant before, but she would always loose the baby in her fourth month. I felt bad for her because she wanted nothing more than be a mother. Everybody loved her including all the cousins and there were many and they were all much younger.

Jack's parents had lots of relatives and they were all close. A few months after I came to America Mike's and Jack's parents moved to a bigger apartment, in the same building were two other sisters of his mom's lived with their families. When we were visiting, there was never a time when the aunts and uncles didn't stop by to say hello, it was always lots of fun.

Chapter 41

WELL, I WENT to work every day and loved my job, though I had to get up early because it took me a long time to get there by train. I had a very nice boss and I got along with all my co-workers. The original six months, I was going to stay, had past and I did not know when I would be able to go home.

I was not happy in my sister's house and we had many disagreements. She was very bossy, and I couldn't take that. I was not the kind of person who likes to argue, so I rather gave in. The only one who kept me sane was Jack; he turned out to become a real good friend. I could confine in him and he understood how I was feeling, and I know he felt sorry for me.

The summer was coming to an end and one day at work; I had such bad stomach pains that I couldn't even stand. My lady friend helped me into the lounge to lie down. It lasted about an hour and then it got better. They wanted me to go to the hospital,l but I did not want to go.

I had signed up to go to night school to get better in English and learn how to read and write and tonight was supposed to be my first day. I still had some pain when I got home and I didn't make it to school, which made me very upset.

When I told my sister, what happen she thought that maybe it was something I ate and hoped that it wouldn't last too long. I was okay for a week and then the pain came back again. I almost passed out and I couldn't understand what was wrong with me.

Everyone told me, to see a doctor but I hated to go, and I was hoping, it will pass again. I thought it had something to do with my periods because I always had bad pain then.

After the third time I did pass out at work and I scheduled an appointment with a doctor. I did not know a doctor, so I went to the family doctor of Jack's parent's and I had to go to Brooklyn to see him. I had no one to take me there, so Jack took off from work and drove me there.

Jack owned his own car now and he was so proud of it. When he bought the car, he asked me if I would mind putting the insurance under my name because it was very expensive for a young guy and he wouldn't be able to afford it.

For me to help him I had to have a learner permit and I needed to take a written test. I told him I was not sure if I could pass the test, I was afraid my English was not good enough. He was always so good to me, so I really wanted to help him.

He took me to the motor vehicle department to schedule the test and I was shocked that I passed the first time because I just guessed the answers. Jack was happy he was able to drive his car, so anytime I needed him for something he would help me, as he did now to take me to the doctor.

He waited outside the office while I went in to see Dr. Castellaneta. He was a very short man and always had to stay on a stool. He examined me and asked me questions and he recommended some tests which he scheduled. I told Jack when I came out and he said he would take me anywhere I had to go.

I haven't had the pain for a while, but I did take the test the doctor ordered, and the outcome was not what I expected because they could not find anything wrong.

He told me then to stay away from spicy food and drink less coffee and he said it could also be stress because I was so homesick. I was puzzled and hoped that was the end of my problem.

Every time I received a letter from my mother I cried, and I was hoping to go home soon. I was getting the pains again on and off and the time was passing by. I did not like the way I looked, I was losing weight and my doctor did not know what was going on. I always looked pale and I could tell Jack was worried. I was happy to have him as my friend because my sister did not seem to care. She hardly ever asks me how I was feeling.

Some months back I decided to dye my hair black, I never liked my original hair color, it was a mousy brown and it was very fine. I liked the new color, but now it made me look even more paler because I was not well. It was already Christmas and my health were not good. I went back and forth to the doctor to take more tests, but they still could not find anything wrong. I was getting very depressed and it showed.

My sister Rene and I were not getting along, and I did not get much sympathy from her while I was not feeling well. Even though I was not looking for any, but I was hoping for some understanding for what I was going through. She was my only relative here and I thought she should have been more supportive.

I wanted to move out and I told Jack, but he said it would not be a good idea for a young girl to live alone.

I was getting frustrated because I was losing time at work by not feeling well and therefore, I was not making enough money so I could save.

Sometimes I couldn't believe how my life had changed since I came to America. I am not even here a year and so much has been going on, especially with my health.

It is now 1963 and I still did not feel any better. Finally, in the beginning of March my doctor told me I had to go into the hospital for more extensive tests, they couldn't do outside, so I did. After two weeks of taking one test after another I was so week and getting sicker, so the doctors decided I needed exploratory surgery. I was so scared and the only one who was with me was Jack.

When I was finally scheduled for the surgery, Jack took off from work to be by my side. I could understand it was hard for Rene to be there after all she did not drive, and she had three small children.

When I woke up from the surgery Jack was in the room and he looked worried. I asked about my sister, he told me he had called her.

When the doctor came in the room, he told me that the problem was that I had adhesions which is scar tissue from a previous operation I had when I was 10 years old and it was not able to be detected with all the other tests.

He also told me that he noticed a lump on my throat, that he was concerned about. I couldn't believe what I was hearing and what was happening to me and I blamed it all on coming here!

Dr. Castellaneta said before I leave the hospital, he wants to take a test regarding my throat. Rene and Mike did come to visit me at the hospital and were very surprised at how I looked.

The doctor told them that when I get home, I would have to watch what I do and especially not to be lifting anything heavy. I could see in Rene's face that she was not happy about that.

Before I left the hospital, the doctor did the test on my neck and he told me that I had several nodules and they need to come out. I was totally against this surgery because I knew a girl from my school who was operated on her neck and she died on the operating table.

The doctor told me, I could wait six months and they would check them again to see if the nodules got bigger, and if that's the case, I would have to have them removed.

I agreed to that because I wanted to concentrate now on getting better and going back to work. Jack came to visit whenever he could, and I was always happy to see him.

I became very fond of him and I think he felt the same about me. When I finally went back to work, my coworkers couldn't believe what I went through. My lady friend did come to see me in the hospital once and I was happy about that. I was so glad to be back at work, but it took me awhile to get back to normal.

I was still very homesick and as soon as anyone would ask me about my mother, I couldn't stop crying.

One day Jack and I visited his sister Rose and she asked me why I was always so sad now. With tears in my eyes I told her that I missed my family very much and that I was saving to go back home but I didn't have enough money yet because I was losing so much time from work.

She said, "why don't you ask Rene and Mike to get you a ticket, but I told her I did not want to ask them because she does not understand."

Rose knew that I had a hard time with Rene, so she offered to lend me the money for the ticket. I told her I could not except that because I would not know when I would be able to pay her back and she said, whenever, would be okay.

I did not want to tell her that I maybe was going back for good, but I think she knew. Even if I was not coming back, I would pay her back because I did not like owing someone money.

I had to first find out from my job if they would give me a leave of absence, if I do decide to come back, at least I would have a job.

When I asked my boss on Monday she said I hate losing you but I will give you the time you need because you went through a lot with your health and seeing your family will probably help you.

Jack and I became very close and we felt that we started to care for each other, more than just being friends and one day he asked me if I wanted to be his girlfriend. I was not ready for that yet and I told him if he still feels the same way when I get back to ask me again.

I had told Rene and Mike about what I wanted to do, and they said whatever I decide is okay with them.

Around the same time when I was planning my trip to go back to Germany, Jack received a letter from the draft board.

He came with me to the airport when I was leaving, and he told me that he would write to me and tell me the outcome regarding the draft.

He also said don't forget what we talked about and that he would not change his mind about me. It made me very sad to say goodbye to him, but I knew I had to see my family in order to get better. I still had a long way to go to be myself again and I hoped going home will help me.

The only one I told that I was coming was my older brother Hans because I had to asked him if I could stay with him and his wife until I decide what to do. I had a good flight back and Hans picked me up from the airport when I arrived.

I was crying and so happy to see him. He lived in Erding (my hometown) with his wife and son Dieter. Hans was now out of the service and he gotten his old job back so they could afford an apartment.

The day after I arrived, I walked to my mother's house and knocked on the door. My mother opened the door and said to me" can I help you." She did not recognize me because I had changed a lot since I left. I had black hair with a different style, and I had lost a lot of weight and besides I still looked somewhat sick.

I said to her "mama it's me, Ingrid" and she was shocked and took me into her arms and we both cried. It felt so good!

INGRID DE MICHELE

She said, what have they done to you and I had to explain everything that happened since I left. She told me that she was never happy when I went to America because after all I was her last daughter.

She also wanted to know what happened with Herbert and I told her what he wrote in the letter. I told her how many letters he wrote to me in the beginning and then suddenly, he wanted to break our engagement.

I told her, that I thought Rene had something to do with it because she always spoke negative about him, but I hope that was not the case.

I told her how great Mike's family is and they are very good to me and that we have dinner at their house every Sunday with the whole family.

My stepfather wanted to know where I was staying and said we do not have any room for you here. Even though my younger brother Freddy was still at home and stayed alone in the same room now, where all our siblings used to sleep.

I would have not stayed there anyway!

Freddy was happy to see me again and I was amazed how tall he gotten in one year. He was almost finished with school and he told me quietly that he had plans to move out as soon as he graduates. He was learning to become a mechanic and was sure he could get a job anywhere.

I have to say my mother looked much better and she told me that she has a good job and I guess that helped. My stepfather was never a good provider, but he always made sure that he always had what he wanted. He was telling me that he was working at a gas station pumping gas and he thought that was a great job. I couldn't care less what he did, as long as he treated my mother well.

I know since I moved away, he became much nicer to her, if she did what he said.

The only thing that upset me a little is, when my mother told me that she developed diabetes and must inject herself twice a day to keep it under control. She said though not to worry about it, she just must watch what she eats!

When I left that day, I told my mom that I don't know what I am going to do yet and how long I was going to stay but I will come and visit again.

I had a conversation with my brother about Jack and told him what a good guy he is, that he always tried to comfort me when I was homesick, and he was on my side when I was so ill. I told him that he asked me to become his girlfriend, but he may be drafted, and I would not want to wait for him living with Rene.

I said it all depended if Jack must go in the service, for me to go back. Then I would only go back until Christmas to see if he was serious about us.

I asked Hans and his wife Rosemarie, if Jack must go away into the service, could I come back and stay with them until I have a job and apartment. They said that would be okay and I was so relieved. I know I had feelings for Jack, and I missed him a lot already, but I did not want to get involved with another soldier, when he must go away from me. Even if I go back and become his girlfriend, I will have to make sure that our feelings towards each other are true.

Chapter 42

I HAD GIVEN Jack my brothers address because he said he would write to me. I was happy being at home, but I also missed him and his family. Two weeks later I received a letter from Jack, telling me that he was rejected from going into the service because of his knees and he was happy. He wanted to know when I was coming back. Now everything will change, and I told Hans what Jack said.

Hans asked me if I still wanted to do what I had told him when I arrived. I asked for his advice and what he would do. He told me, "I don't know Jack but from all the things you told me about him, he must be a good guy."

I had told him also how loving Mike and Jack's family are and if I and Jack should get together, I think his family would be happy. At least that is what I thought, they always tried to help me when I was not happy living with Rene.

I went to my mother's house many times to spend time with her, we also went sometimes to the ice cream parlor because we both liked ice cream and I wanted to spend time alone with her.

She told me how sorry she was for what we went through as children, but she felt she had no other choice. She said that her husband gotten better since all of us were gone. I really did not want to talk about that anymore and I wanted to tell her about my plans.

She was sorry to hear that I was planning to leave again but she understood I had to try, if I had feelings for Jack! I told her she would like him; he has a good heart and that his family is great. It made her happy to hear that, but I also told her if it wouldn't work out, I will be back.

I had also visited my father and his wife and told them all about how my life was until now in the united states and when I said goodbye, they wished me the best of luck

I set a date for my return and I let Rene and Mike know when I was coming back. I did not give them the real reason why, but they did say I could stay with them again.

If I get my old job back which I was hoping, I will save so I could pay back Rose and maybe I could get a room somewhere.

I let Jack know when I was arriving and he told me, he would pick me up. I was so happy to see him and when he walked up to me, he kissed me on my mouth for the first time and he gave me a long hug, like he never wanted me to leave again. My heart started to beat very fast!

He drove me home and Mike and Rene and the children seemed happy to see me. Baby Patricia was already a year old and she was so cute as was little Cathy. They both looked like two little dolls with curly hair. Cathy had blond curls and Patricia's were dark!

The following day I called my job and spoke to my boss and she said I could come back as soon as I was ready, and I started the next Monday. I was so happy to be there, and she even gave me a small raise. My lady friend said, "you look like the trip did you good, you look much healthier" and I agreed.

Everything went back to the same routine, except I told Rene that I needed more time for myself and if she wanted me to babysit she would have to let me know ahead of time and if I had no other plans I would be happy to do it.

Jack told me that he has a better job and making a little more money and therefore we could go out more. We double dated many times with his best friend Guy and his girlfriend Millie, and we had lots of fun even though they both argued every time.

He did not mention or asked me to be his girlfriend again, but I knew all his friends thought I was. He never went out with anyone else.

INGRID DE MICHELE

One day, towards the end of August, Jack told me not to make any plans for the weekend, he wanted to take me out. We never went anywhere fancy because he did not make that much money and I was just happy to be with him. Wherever we went though was fine with me!

That day he picked me up and he looked so handsome and we drove to Brooklyn and parked at plum beach. I heard about plum beach before, all the young guys used to bring their dates there, when they wanted to be alone.

We parked in the lot and just talked. He told me he came here many times with a girl, but he was getting older and he doesn't need to that anymore. I was too shy to ask what he meant but I had an idea. He asked me if I was sorry that I came back and could I see myself living here for good. I told him that my life would have to change much for the better.

He asked me to open the glove compartment in the car and I did. There was a box laying in there and he asked me to take it out.

He asks me to open it and when I did, I saw a gold bracelet with two little hearts on it. I was getting nervous because I thought he bought that for a girl. He asked me if I liked it and if I knew what it was. I said not really, and he wanted me to take it out and look at it closer.

I saw that one heart said Jack and the other Ingrid and todays date. I knew it meant something special and I asked him what it meant.

He explained that when a guy wants to go steady with a girl, then he gives her an ankle bracelet that she wears on her ankle. I did not know that, because I never met anyone who wore one, or I never paid attention.

I thought it was sweet and the whole time he had this big smile on his face. He said to me" Ingrid, I love you and I only want to be with you, and would you wear it for me". I was so touched that it made me cry and naturally I said yes!

I was really surprised and very happy. I thanked him and he helped me put it on. We stayed there for a while and started kissing or how all his friends called it," making out." I knew I loved him too and all I could think about, how my life will change now, and I hoped with all my heart that nothing will happen to change, how happy I was at that moment!

I was wondering what my sister Rene would say!

As we were driving home, Jack talked about the future and said he is going to look for a better job. When we got home Rene and Mike were out and our neighbor was babysitting. We told her she could go home; we would take over.

I did not get to tell Rene until the following day, and she did not say anything. I asked her if she knew what it meant, and she said yes. My lady friend at work was more excited than my own sister, which I still cannot understand.

Didn't she want me to be happy?

INGRID DE MICHELE

Every morning when I got ready for work and looked in the mirror, I would notice that the lump on my neck looked larger. Even when I told Jack he said he had noticed too and told me to see Dr. Castellaneta. I made an appointment for two weeks later and Jack came with me. The doctor measured my neck and he said it grew 6cm and he informed me that they must come out.

I was getting nervous, but he assured me that it will be okay. We set date for early October and again Jack stood by my side and took me to the hospital. On the day of the operation he was also nervous, but he stayed at the hospital until he was able to see me.!

The surgery went well but I had a very sore throat. The doctor told me that he removed three nodules and one was very close to my throat, that is why I had trouble swallowing.

Well, now I must recuperate again, so I could go back to work as soon as possible

I told Jack, I hope this is the end of my operations, two in one year is too many? I was out of work for two weeks and my boss was glad everything went well. I was so lucky to have her as my boss; she was a nice lady and liked me a lot.

I written my mother a letter and to Hans and told them, that it looks like I was not coming back to Germany just yet. Before Christmas I was finally paying back the money I had borrowed from Rose and I thanked her again.

She was happy about Jack and me and so was his sister Millie and his parents. They all said that they thought Jack had feelings for me.

Jack and I did not go out much anymore, he said he had to save money and I could understand that because I did the same. He was spending enough money on gas to come back and forth to see me and we were just happy to see each other on his day off.

Christmas came and we were all together with his family. Jack's father was very much into the holidays and his whole house was decorated. Many decorations he made himself and they were beautiful! It made me think about my Christmases growing up as a child and I was so happy being with Jack and those years were over!

He gave me a beautiful bracelet for Christmas, and he called it a charm bracelet and he said, I will add to it on different occasions.

On New Year's Eve we wanted to go to New York city with friends, but it was so cold outside that we decided to go to a restaurant instead. I bought myself a new dress and Jack told me how nice I looked.

One of the girls wanted some coffee and when she picked it up it slipped out of her hand and it landed all over my new dress. I was very upset, because not only was my dress now covered with coffee, but I also got burned and therefore wanted to go home. I hoped that the stain will come out! We had a long way to the train station, and it was even colder now.

INGRID DE MICHELE

I didn't expect to start 1964 this way!

It was winter, so there was not much to do, except going to work every day. We saw each other whenever possible. I was still unhappy with my living situation and constantly told Jack that I wanted to move out, but he did not like me living somewhere alone and said just wait, it will get better. Every time we were together, he always talked about getting a better job and he asked his brother Mike to get him an application for Pan American. Mike told him; he may have to start at the bottom, but Jack did not care because the benefits would be good.

One day in February Jack came to my job to pick me up and I was surprised to see him there because he usually tells me when he comes. I asked him why he came, and he said I want to take you somewhere after work.

So, when I was done with work, we left and walked towards the train station, like I always did but he said let's walk down the street.

It was very cold outside, and I was wondering why he was not in a hurry to get home. He stopped at a jewelry store and he said, let's go in. I had no clue why he wanted to go in there but naturally I followed him. Once we were in the store, someone came over and asked if he could help us. Jack told him that he wanted to see some engagement rings. I could not believe what he was saying, and my heart was pounding, and I was nervous!

He told me that he just wanted to get an idea what kind of stone or ring I liked, when he was able to afford to buy me one.

The man showed us many rings and I thought, they all were beautiful. I did not want him to spend his money on a ring for me. He showed me, what they called a princess cut and asked me if I liked it. I told him then, it does not matter what I like, I did not need a ring with a diamond, this was all new to me.

As I said before, in Germany when a couple gets engaged and plan to marry, they buy a set of rings together either in gold or silver and wear it on the left hand and when they get married, they switch the ring to the right hand. So, for me, to get a diamond engagement ring was not necessary. When we left the store and where on our way home, Jack told me, that I should be happy if he wanted to buy me a diamond ring because that is what a man does for the girl he loves and wants to marry.

He said, his family always told him, that was the right thing to do!

Naturally it made me very happy and I could not believe how lucky I was to have found Jack and that he loves me! It looks like my life in this country will finally get much better!

He also told me that he spoke to his brother Mike about getting a job at Pan American airways and he said he would help him. Soon after that Mike brought him an application and not long after that he was called in to take a test, which he past and he was to start his new job on April first. I was so happy for him.

INGRID DE MICHELE

At the end of February after my 21st birthday we were all at his house with Rene and Mike and their children. Jack told me that he had something for me and on front of his family he presented me with an engagement ring and asked me to marry him.

I was so surprised that he already had bought the ring, but I could not have been happier. The ring was a princess cut and so beautiful. His parents were very happy, and his father said, we must have a party and he offered to pay for it and the planning started.

Chapter 43

MY FUTURE FATHER -in law was very funny and said to me ," Ingrid I feel sorry for you if you marry my son, because he is so picky with everything he eats and I wish you luck", but I did not care about that.

I loved him very much!

Just before Jack started his new job, we had a beautiful engagement party and we received so many presents. I met all of Jack's family there and I was able to invite some of my friends from work, my lady friend was especially happy for me when she found out.

I wished, my mother could have been there, she would be so happy for me, but I will write and send pictures to her and tell her everything. I always hoped and dreamed that one day I will have a better life and I think it is starting to come true.

I always said if I should marry someone who is of catholic religion, that I would convert. When I lived with my friend Loni in Munich I always went to catholic church with her. So, I told his parents that I would register for religious instructions at their church and that made them happy.

Jack and I talked about when we should get married and because I always dreamed of being a June bride, we decided to set a date of June 1965.

Jack was happy at his new job and he did a lot of schooling to advance himself. From the day we got engaged Jack and I made many plans for our life together.

We knew it was important to save our money now for the wedding and therefore didn't go out much. Jack spend his days off with me and we would take a drive to the park or beach in the summer, which was fine with me.

We talked about who we would want to invite to the wedding. I told him that I didn't think that my family would be able to afford to come, so there will be only Rene on my side and maybe a few friends. I guess it would mostly be Jack's family and whoever his parents would want to invite.

There was so much to think about planning a wedding and I did not know anything about it. I had to rely on Jack's family to help me.

We were told that we should look at some halls first so we could get the date we wanted, even though it was more than a year away. Jack knew lots of places and we decided to go on weekends to check them out.

Since I have been together with Jack, we had gone to two weddings, when his friends got married and to me, they were amazing. At his best friend's Guy and his fiancée Millie's wedding we were asked to be attendants, which was all new to me and made me very nervous, but I enjoyed every minute.

After several weekends looking at some places for our wedding we found one that we both liked, and we asked Jack's parents to come and look at it with us.

The place was called "Pisa" and it was in Brooklyn and my future in – laws loved it. So, we were able to book it for June 19th of 1965 and I was so happy. We had to put down a deposit to hold it and they told us that when the time comes closer, we would have to pick out a menu for the dinner.

I could not believe this was all for my wedding that I dreamed about!

Jack and I spent every free time we had together, and we made lots of plans. I noticed that Rene never asked me anything about the wedding and I could not understand why. She was the only family I had here, and I wanted her to be happy for me. The months passed by quickly because we were very busy.

Jack thought we should look at some bedroom furniture and when he mentioned it to his parents, they offered to give us

$2000 dollars towards the purchase, as a wedding gift. I was very thankful for their generosity.

There were many furniture stores in Brooklyn, and we went to all of them, until we found something we liked and placed on order. My lady friend at work was always very excited for me when I told her what we were doing, more so then my sister!

One day she asked me what kind of wedding dress I think I would like? There was a bridal shop across the street, and she told me "why don't you go in there and look at some of the dresses, so you get an idea." There was a dress in the window that I thought was beautiful. It had lots of lace and a very full skirt with more lace.

So, one day after work I went in there and I told them what I was looking for. The lady asked me when I was getting married and I told her, and she said that I was not to early and I should try on several dresses to see what I liked. I said, I would like to try on the dress in the window and when I put it on, I thought I looked like a princess and fell in love with it.

They even gave me a headpiece to try on with the dress and I thought I was dreaming, which brought tears to my eyes.

I was crying because I should have been able to do this with my mother or at least with my sister, but she never offered to come with me, when I asked her. The sales lady told me if I really wanted this dress, I should put a deposit down and when the time comes closer, she would put the order in, but I still had time.

My future sister in-law Rose worked as a seamstress and she asked me one day if I had any idea what kind of wedding dress I would like. I told her what I did, and she thought I should look a little more. She knew a lot of wedding dress factories in New York through her job and she offered to take me there one weekend. Besides she said they probably be much cheaper, and I could make any changes I would want.

I already knew that the bride should have bridesmaids and because I did not have any friends to ask, I decided to ask Jack's cousin's Patricia and Barbara, who lived in the same building as Jack and they were happy and said, yes. Even though my sister was not very into my upcoming Wedding, I would have never considered asking anyone else to be my maid of honor, and Jack ask his brother Mike to be his best man.

Rose thought, that it would be good if the whole bridal party would get together one day and see about bridesmaid dresses to. So, we picked a weekend and went into the city and visited several factories. When I walked into one of the places, there were rack's and racks of wedding dresses. One had caught my eye and Rose said to me" remember Ingrid, whatever you don't like about the dress you can ask them to change it".

The dress I looked at had short sleeves and I wanted long sleeves, even though the wedding was in June. So, I tried it on, and I loved it more than the one I had a deposit on. The lady told me there will be no problem adding long sleeves. I also

INGRID DE MICHELE

wanted the lace to go all the way down the skirt. The dress was beautiful, and it had a long train, that I loved. Also, it was 200 dollars cheaper, buy buying it wholesale. I was glad I listened to Rose!

We even found bridesmaid dresses that Rene and the girls picked out. They chose a light blue color and Rene's was a little darker, which was fine with me. I thanked Rose for taking me there and she promised to come along for the fittings.

The time flew by and we celebrated another Christmas. Jack gave me a beautiful charm for my bracelet. It was a large heart locket with little pearls going around it and a diamond in the middle, I loved it. I considered myself so lucky to be his girl and he was so good to me.

Everything was going along well with the wedding preparations and three months before the wedding we started looking for a place to live. We wanted to be near a train for me to go to work and that Jack is not so far away from the airport. He was so happy at his job and he got some promotions which meant more money and that was a good thing.

Jack asked me one day, where should we go on a honeymoon and he said because he is already working a year at Pan American airways, we were able to fly anywhere with a good discount but we would have to fly stand by which means if there are seats available, we will get on the flight.

So, he said to me how would you like to go to Hawaii? Never in my life, did I ever think, that I would have a chance to go to Hawaii. Again, another one of my dreams seems to be coming true.

He is making me so happy!

I could not wait to become Jack's wife, I loved him so much!

In March I received an invitation to go to a bridal shower for Jack's cousin's fiancée, who was getting married a week after us.

Weeks before, I decided to let my black hair grow out because I wanted to have my natural color back. My hair does not grow fast, and I was getting impatient. So, I went to the beauty parlor and asked them to do something. They told me that they had to strip my hair first to get the black out and then color it to match my own. I told them if my hair does not turn red, to go ahead.

When my hair was done, I was a strawberry red and I was upset. She didn't want to put more color on it and told me that I would have to wait at least two weeks, then we would try something else.

Well, in two weeks was that shower and there would be a lot of people who knew me only with black hair, so I decided to dye it black again. I hated the color now and Jack didn't like it either.

At that time, I was very sad because my sister and I had a big fight and I did not talk to her for some time. I felt that she was jealous of all the good things that was happening in my life.

So, when the day of the shower came, I knew Rene would be there. Jack drove me there and we were a little late and I asked Jack to go in with me. I walked in first and I got so scared because everyone screamed surprise and I turned around, I thought the bride was behind me, but there was only Jack.

His sister Rose came over to me and said" I am so glad you are surprised because this is your shower".

Jack gave me a kiss and hug and told me to have a great time and I should stop crying! I could not believe this was all done for me. Rose looked kind of upset because she made me a bride doll and she tried to match my hair and there I was again with black hair. She said to me" do you know how many dolls there are with black hair", I said I'm sorry.

First, I started to say hello to all the people, and it was mostly Jack's family and I saw Jack's cousin's fiancée, who I thought the shower was for. When I saw that some of my coworkers were there, I was surprised and happy.

Naturally my sister was there, and she walked up to me and gave me a hug and said, I'm sorry!

My shower was great, and I had a good time, I received so many beautiful gifts including the gift I brought. Someone made a big hat with all the ribbons of the gifts and placed it on my head, it looked funny but nice. They also made us play games where they wrote everything down what I said, and it turned out real funny. I never seen anything like it!

When it was over Jack came back to pick me up, he saw how happy I was, and I showed him all the beautiful gifts. I told him; I don't think we need to buy anything for our house. I did not know how everyone who was there knew what we could use, but I think it was my in-laws who told them?

We asked a few relatives if they could take some of the things for us in their car to bring them to Jack's parents' house to store, until we have an apartment.

Soon after the shower we found an apartment in Ridgewood Queens on the fourth floor. It needed some fixing up and we wanted to paint the rooms. It had one bedroom, living room and an eat-in kitchen with a bath. We had fun doing all the work ourselves, whenever we had free time.

I loved my future father in-law and I had planned to ask him to walk me down the aisle. When I mentioned it to Rene, she informed me that she asked my father, if he would like to come to America for the wedding, so he could give me away and he said yes.

I know Rene was much closer to my father than me so I could understand that she wanted him here, but I was not very happy about that because if anyone should come, then it should be my mother. She is the one who raised me, but I couldn't say anything, Rene and Mike were paying for the ticket and I did not want to upset them or get into a fight before my wedding, but I wished they would have asked me for my opinion!

Now it was time to pick out the menu for the wedding, we took Jack's parents with us to the hall to help us decide what we should have. I would have had no idea!

One month before our wedding date, I was baptized and received confirmation in the catholic church, and I had asked Jack's sister Millie to be my godmother. Father John gave me the religious instructions and I liked him very much, so we wanted him to perform our wedding ceremony. He was transferred though two weeks before and they would not let him come to the church, which made me sad, he was so nice.

Few weeks before the wedding we all went for our final fitting for our dresses and they all came out okay and we were able to take them home.

My dress was so beautiful, and I was so happy that Rose told me to go there. I brought my dress to Rose's house because I was planning to get dressed at her house. I also brought my headpiece there the same day!

Everything was going well; we finished our apartment and we were waiting for our bedroom furniture to be delivered. It came a week before, but they told us that my dresser will be delayed but promised we would get it when we come back from our honeymoon. We also had ordered a couch for the living room and that came on time. We had no money to buy a coffee table so Jack found a strong box and I put a nice tablecloth over it, and we will use it until we could afford something else.

We had also brought all the gifts we had received from the engagement and shower to our place and I put everything were it belonged.

Sometime ago, a friend of Rene's was moving back to Germany for good because she did not like it in America, and she was selling everything. Rene told her that I was getting married and she thought maybe I could use some of her things.

I went there with Rene and she had a beautiful Bavarian elf-enbein with a gold rim china dish set, service for twelve and it was in great condition. She wanted only fifty dollars and I had to buy it for that price. It was well worth it!

I could not believe that she didn't want to take it with her.

I was so excited fixing up our new place I couldn't wait to live there with him, but I was also getting nervous, I did not want to disappoint him!

We had also brought our clothes to the apartment and kept aside what we needed for our honeymoon. I bought a few new things and couldn't wait to wear them and show Jack!

INGRID DE MICHELE

A few days before our big day, we packed our luggage for the honeymoon and brought them to Rose's house because we were leaving from there. We were going to stay in a hotel by the airport that night for the trip the next day.

We had taken care of our marriage license. We had to go downtown Brooklyn for that, and I thought how different everything is here, then in Germany, the couple must go on front of the mayor first to get married, before they could go to church.

All I could think of, whatever it takes for me to marry Jack, I will do even if it seemed strange to me.

Chapter 44

***

WELL, THE DAY of my wedding was finally here. I stayed the night before at Jack's parents' house and he stayed at his sisters.

I was going there after I had my hair and make-up done and he would be gone by then and go back to his mothers. I did not know that we should not see each other that day, until I walk down the aisle in church.

I was getting really very nervous!

When I was done at the hairdressers, I took a taxi to Rose's house and the driver said to me, you look very nice are you getting married today and I said yes. He said well, then the ride is on me. When he dropped me of at the house, I thanked him, and he wished me good luck.

When I walked in, Rose asked me if I was hungry, but I said I'm too nervous to eat but she made me something anyway.

I still had time to get ready, the church service was not until 4 pm. Rene and Mike, who was Jack's best man with the children and my father were going to arrive by 2pm. The day started out sunny and when my father and the others arrived it started to rain. Rose said to me don't worry a little rain on your wedding day means good luck.

Mike did not stay, he had to be at Jack's house and one of the limo drivers brought him there. It did not rain very long, and the sun came back out again. The photographer had arrived, and Rene and Rose helped me get dressed and put on my vail. When I first picked out my vail, I really wanted a very long vail but Rose thought it would hide my beautiful train on my dress, so I chose one to my elbows.

When I looked in the mirror, I could not believe it was me. Since I got up this morning until now, I keep on thinking I must be dreaming.

The photographer started to take lots of pictures with all of us there, some with my father and Rene also Rene's daughter Cathy who was the flower girl. I can't wait to see all the pictures!

The cars we hired, to take us to the church and hall had arrived and we were ready to leave.

They had just opened the road for the new Verrazano bridge, so we got to the church a little early. I told the driver to wait on the side block before the church because I knew there was another wedding going on.

As we were standing there, the church doors opened, and the priest came out and waved us over. The driver moved the car to the front of the church steps, and someone came over and told us there was no wedding now because the groom never showed up and they were ready for us.

I thought what a terrible thing for that bride and I hoped with all my heart that Jack will be there.

We all got out of the car and walked up the stairs. I saw a lot of people we knew coming in to see us get married. They made us stand on the side of the doors and someone told me that Jack is already there, I was so relieved. I was so nervous I was shaking, I also worried about walking down the aisle, I didn't want to trip, it was a long aisle.

My bridesmaids looked so pretty and the flowers we had ordered were beautiful especially my bouquet.

One of the men came and put down a long white runner, the whole length of the aisle and told us everyone is ready. I heard the music playing and the photographer was going to guide us in. The doors opened and the bridesmaids started to walk in with the usher's Jack had chosen. Then the flower girl walked in just ahead of Rene. When the organ played "here comes the bride" it was my time to walk down the aisle with my father.

INGRID DE MICHELE

The whole time I thought I was dreaming!

Jack was standing by the altar waiting for me, he looked so handsome!

When we reached the altar, my father lifted my vail and gave me a kiss and put my hand into Jack's and together we walked up the altar. Jack whispered in my year" you look so beautiful." The priest noticed how I was shaking and he said to me in a very heavy Italian accent" what's the matter with you, do you want to change your mind" and I just shook my head and said" no", and the ceremony began.

It was the most beautiful and touching ceremony, especially when someone started to sing the song" Ave Maria" while we were exchanging our vows.

I considered myself the luckiest girl in the world and now I'm becoming Jack's wife.

I was on cloud nine and very, very happy!

When the ceremony was over, Jack and I kissed and then walked to the front of the church and all the people lined up and wished us all the best.

The photographer took lots more pictures inside and outside the church and before we went to the hall, we went to the studio with the whole bridal party to take more. We did not have to be at the hall until after 5 pm. The cocktail hour started at six for the guests and we had our own in a suite.

Everyone started walking into the hall around seven and the band started introducing the bridal party and then us. When he said now for the first time, we welcome Mr. and Mrs. Jack De Michele, I couldn't have been happier.

The song we picked for our first dance was from the movie westside story which we liked at that time!

There were so many people at our wedding that I did not know, but Jack and I walked from table to table and greeted everyone and thanked them for coming. Most of the time I did not know what was going on because I still thought I was in my dream, I just always followed Jack.

At one point, when I was on the way to the bathroom, I passed my father in-law as he was talking to Jack's uncle and he called me over. He said to me," Ingrid I want you to witness something". Uncle Sal took out his wallet and gave him ten dollars and said, you win.

I did not know what they were talking about, but he explained that when I first came to this country and he got to know me, he made a bet with him that Jack was going to marry me. I couldn't believe it, but it made me very happy that he thought then already, I was good for his son. I gave him a kiss and said, "I am so glad that you were right".

Everyone was having a great time and the wedding was supposed to be over by 11pm. My father in-law saw that no one wanted to leave, and he told Jack, that he would like to extend it for another hour, and he offered to pay for it.

For me, the whole day was a dream and all my wishes came finally true!

When the party was over, we settled the account and said goodbye to everyone, including my father because he was going back to Germany, before we come back from our honeymoon.

We drove to Rose's house and once we got changed, we took our luggage and Rose and her husband drove us to the hotel by the airport.

I had asked Rose to come up to the room because I was nervous, but she told me not to worry everything will be okay.

I told myself why you are nervous, Jack is your husband now and I am his wife.

The next morning the phone rang, and it was my mother in-law and she asked my husband if he is okay and he told her, yes, when he hung up, we both laughed

.

When we got to the airport our first flight was with delta to Atlanta and then to continue to San Francisco and Hawaii. We were flying stand bye so already we were not able to get on the first flight to San Francisco and we were bumped until the last flight. Once we got to San Francisco we had to stay over and continue our flight to Hawaii the next day.

When we finally arrived on the island it looked so beautiful. As we came of the plane there were girls and boys who greeted us with a flowered lie.

We had a great time on our honeymoon. We visited all the other islands on a small plane who were also very nice with lots of flowers and orchids.

We couldn't have had a better honeymoon; it was two wonderful weeks!

INGRID DE MICHELE

Chapter 45

NOW, WE WERE back home, and our life together started. The first Sunday home, I wanted to cook my new husband a good Italian meal (spaghetti and meatballs). I had watched my sister how to make it. I had everything prepared and, in the pot, when everyone called to find out about our honeymoon.

I was not paying attention to the sauce and it burned.

I was so upset and started crying. When Jack saw what happened, he took me in his arms and kissed me and said don't worry honey, we will go out to eat. I was so grateful that he wasn't mad!

I thought to myself, this is how a marriage should be, not like my mother's, who had to constantly be on guard with my stepfather.

On the top floor of our apartment building lived three more

couples who were also newlyweds. The ones next to us, Jean and John were very nice, and we became friends. Jack and John had a lot to talk about because they both worked for an airline. Jean worked for a company in New York city.

I still worked in Jamaica Queens and I had to take several trains to get there. I told Jack I wanted to get a job closer to the house because we hardly saw each other, he worked nightshift and me during the day, which was not good for newlyweds?

A few months later I found a job around the corner of our house at the supermarket, as a cashier and when I told my boss that I was leaving, she was sad but understood.

I was working at my new job a few months when Jean told me that her company was looking for someone in the customer service department. I told her that I never done that kind of work, but she told me if you get the job, someone will train you. She arranged an interview for me and when I went there, they liked me and offered me the position. I thanked Jean and I was happy to make more money. I started two weeks later, and Jack was happy for me!

One night we invited my in-laws for dinner, and I decided to make roast beef because I heard him say one day that he liked it. When dinner was over, my father-in law said "Ingrid this was the best roast beef I ever ate, and it made me feel really good!

INGRID DE MICHELE

Soon, it was going to be our first Christmas together as husband and wife. It was lots of fun buying our first Christmas tree and the decorations. We even bought a small tree for the fire escape outside our kitchen window. Jack put lights on it, so you could see it from the street. We decorated the apartment and it looked very festive; we had a very nice first Christmas together.

It was now the beginning of 1966 and I realized that I had missed two of my periods. Jack wanted me to see a doctor and his sister Rose recommended one in Brooklyn, that she used. We made an appointment and went to see him. He examined me and told us; it looks like you are going to have a baby. He gave me some vitamins and said take care of yourself and gave me another appointment for later.

Jack and I were very happy, and we couldn't wait to tell his parents!

Jean, my neighbor, congratulated me and said, I hope I will soon become pregnant too. I had a great job and soon I will be a mother, I was happy!

Jack was able to change his work shift and now we had more time together. We decided to look for a two-bedroom apartment and found one not far from the old one. It was a private house and the owners were from Germany. Jean and John were sorry we moved but we got together on weekends.

I saw Jean every day at work and we also rode the train together.

We only lived in our new apartment two months when one night I started to get bad cramps and I was bleeding. Jack called the doctor and he prescribed some medication. He also told us to watch the bleeding because I may lose the baby. I was getting upset but there was nothing I could do. Jack went to get the medicine for me and nothing more happen that night except my cramps and the bleeding didn't stop.

I went to see the doctor the following day and I told him that the bleeding was just like a period. He wanted to examine me anyway and I felt so uncomfortable. When it was over, he told us that it looks like I was never pregnant, and I had a false pregnancy. I did not understand but he explained that when someone is very anxious to get pregnant the body does crazy things. I couldn't believe what he was saying because I never heard of a false pregnancy before.

When Jean found out, she was surprised to hear that and when I went back to work, I did not know what to say, but Jean said she would talk to everyone. Jack and I were very disappointed about the whole thing and he said to me, let's not worry about having a baby so much, if god wants us to have a family, it will happen.

As the months passed, we decided to take a trip to Germany for our first wedding anniversary. I wanted my family to meet Jack. I also wanted to take our wedding films with us so everyone could see them. I contacted my brother Hans to see if he has room for us and he answered that we were welcome in his house. He was excited to meet Jack!

INGRID DE MICHELE

I told him that I would like to invite the whole family for a little party so we all could watch the movies together. He told me that would be nice but did not know if both of our parents will come because my stepfather does not like to be in the same room as my father. They have not been in the same room since my brother's wedding, but I told him that I would talk to them, and I would be disappointed if they don't come.

When we finally got to Germany, I was happy to be home again and when I told them what I have planned, they all said they would come. So, the night of the party everyone from my family came and we had a good time. When we showed the movies, my mother had tears in her eyes and told me, I wished I was there instead of your father and I said, me too.

Everyone told me that they liked Jack and that made me happy!

While I was there, my father told me that there is a dance coming up near his house the following weekend, and he asked us if we wanted to come. Hans and Rosie were going too, so we all said yes. When we got there, my father's wife did not come, which surprised me, but he told me she does not like to dance.

There were lots of people there and some of my brother's friends, I knew from years ago. Some of them asked me to dance and when I asked Jack, he said okay.

When I danced a polka with one of the guys, he had his hand on my back a little lower than Jack liked and so he went to the guy and told him to get his hands of his wife. My father did not like that, and he came over and told me, Jack should not have done that, and he is nothing like his brother Mike and thought I made a mistake by marrying him.

I was so mad at him for saying that and told him, I love him, and he is a good man and you have no right to say anything about my husband.

Soon after that our vacation was over, and we had to say good-bye to everyone.

We were lucky that Jack had a good job in the airlines which made us able to fly more often. While he was working, he took many classes to get a better positions and better pay. When he finally went for his A & P license, he had to go to Texas for a week to take the test.

He passed and I was so proud of him!

I enjoyed being Jack's wife and every day was a special day for us. We spent almost every Sunday with his family and his sisters, and their husband's would be there too. There was always lots of laughs. Just before thanksgiving my sister in-law Millie announced that she was pregnant. She had several miscarriages, so we were worried. They were already married 13 years and really wanted a child. She was using the same doctor I had and so far, everything looked good.

In 1967 my father -in law started to get sick and we were all worried.

Millie's pregnancy went well and in July she gave birth to a

178   INGRID DE MICHELE

baby girl. My father in-law was in the hospital at that time and when she planned the christening, we asked the doctors if he could come out for the event, which they said okay.

My in-laws were very happy about the baby, they always hoped that their daughters would have a child.

I thought to myself, maybe it was not my time to have a baby but instead it was hers and my time will come.

Jack and I planned another trip and we wanted to go to Europe in August. About a month before we left, we had gone back to the doctor because my periods were so irregular. He told Jack, before we do extreme testing on your wife, I want to check your sperm count, which he did, and it came back low. We told him that we were going away for a month on vacation and he said, go and enjoy yourself, we will take care of it when you come back.

Our plan was to fly to Paris for a few days, then to Rome, stay there for a while and then to see Italy. After Italy we wanted to go to Vienna. When we arrived in Paris, I just loved it, to me it was a very romantic city. I also liked Rome, but it was very old and had lots of ruins, but it was interesting seeing such an ancient city.

While we were in Rome, we decided to go to the island of Capri, but had to stay overnight in Sorrento. The hotel was beautiful and brand new and all made of Italian marble.

The next day we went to Capri and I wanted to take the boat ride into the grotto. The boat was small, and it was rocking quiet a bid. I became sick to my stomach and Jack asked me if I wanted to get off, but I said no. After a while I started to feel better and enjoyed myself. The following day we had to go back to Rome to get ready for our flight to Vienna.

We also loved Vienna and we saw all the sights. There at least, I was able to speak German and that helped. One night we went to the opera house to see a play and even though Jack did not understand much, he still liked it. We were there for three nights and our last flight was to Munich to see my family again.

I felt so lucky that I was able to travel with Jack like that. When I grew up in Germany, I never went anywhere. I was glad that Jack enjoyed it too, because he never traveled much before either.

We knew that the Oktoberfest would be on in Munich while we were there, and Jack really wanted to go and see it. We stayed with my brother Hans again and by now he had already three children. Two boys and one daughter who was only six months old and very cute. They were so happy to finally have a little girl!

Every time I came to Germany, I would bring some presents for everyone and they were grateful for it.

We visited all the family and one weekend we went by train to Munich to the Oktoberfest. Jack was amazed how big it was; there were lots of rides and many beer tents with German bands playing.

I did not like going on rides, but Jack talked me into going on some. One of those rides you had to stand against the wall while it went up and down and around real fast. As it was coming to a stop, I lost my footing and slid right across the other side. I slammed into something with my body and I was sore the next day.

My brother Freddy had moved away from home and he was not living close, so I did not get to see him on this visit. Our vacation was coming to an end and again we had to say goodbye to my family. It always was hard for me, especially saying goodbye to my mother.

Chapter 47

ONCE WE GOT back home, we both had to go back to work. When I saw Jean at work, she told me that she was pregnant and was due the end of April. I was happy for her and thought, I hope I can say that soon too.

It was the end of October when I realized that I did not have my period since I left on vacation. I told Jack and he asked me if I wanted to go to the doctor, but I told him no, that I wanted to wait.

Another month passed and I noticed that I was always nauseous in the morning riding the train to work.

I was sick to my stomach a lot on vacation, but I did not pay much attention. I also noticed that my clothes were getting kind of tight and I had a slight belly, but I still did not want to go to the doctor.

Finally, when I missed my fourth cycle, I made an appointment. When I saw him, he examined me and took a blood test, he confirmed that I was four months pregnant and he said we will hear the heartbeat soon.

He wanted to see me in another month and again I needed to take vitamins. Jack told him I guess my sperm count wasn't so low after all.

When we left the office, I told Jack that I did not want to tell anyone just yet until I hear the heartbeat and he agreed.

We went on with our everyday life and didn't think so much about the pregnancy. I could not eat breakfast before I went to work because I always became sick to my stomach and I did not want to vomit on the train. So, I lived on saltine crackers, because they helped.

We celebrated our second Christmas and it was very nice except we all were worried about Jack's father. They found out that he had cancer and it was very aggressive. He was in and out of the hospital not doing well at all.

In January I went back to the doctor and he told me there is no mistake this time, you are pregnant, but he still couldn't hear the heartbeat, which worried me. We still did not say anything to anyone. Finally , when I saw the doctor the following month, he heard the heartbeat and he made me and Jack listen.

We were both happy and relieved. I told the doctor that I feel I have butterflies in my belly, and he said that would be the baby moving and it will get stronger!

Already I felt so much love for this baby and even more for Jack!

After we left the office, we drove to Jack's parents' house and told them about the baby. They were very excited and happy for us; they knew how much we wanted a child.

I also called my sister Rene and Mike and let them know. Instead of saying congratulations Rene said, "it's about time, I thought you didn't know how to do it". I was shocked that she would even say something like that!

My morning sickness was getting better and I was glad about that, but I started to feel tired by the end of the day. Jack was a very attentive husband and helped me with everything when he was at home.

We did not want to buy anything for the baby yet, but we did paint the second bedroom. When we were out, we just look at things we would need for the baby and see what we liked.

Now Jean and I had a lot to talk about our upcoming baby arrival. She was due one month ahead of me and she told me that they were looking for a house on Long Island, NY. Jack and I were planning to do the same soon, but right now we have enough room, when the baby arrives.

The months flew by and the doctor told us the baby will come in the beginning of May. I had to see him more often now and then in April I saw him once a week.

He always assured us that everything is going well. Jean left her job at the end of march and in April she had a baby boy!

Jack's sister Rose had purchased a house near her other sister's house and one weekend they invited us. When we got there most of his family was there for a baby shower for us. We received so many lovely gifts which will be able to use soon.

Every time something so nice happens to me; I can't believe how lucky I am and how my life is so wonderful now!

I worked at my job until 4 weeks before my due date and everyone wished me good luck when I left. I loved my job and was sorry to leave, but I know I won't miss the everyday train ride.

When my time came close, Jack and I stayed at his parents' house because it was closer to the hospital.

Also, my father in-law was again in the hospital and he was very sick.

I was already two weeks passed my due date and I was getting anxious. My mother in -law was very protective and wouldn't let me go anywhere but I know she meant well.

One day when Jack came home from work, I begged him to take a walk with me after dinner. I had to get out of the house for a while. We took a long walk and I was exhausted when

I got back but it helped because that night, I started getting pains in my back. First, I thought that can't be labor pains because all the pain was in my back, but when it got stronger, I woke up Jack to call the doctor.

Jack was so worried when he took me to the hospital. When I got there the doctor examined me and he thought the baby was breeched and he ordered an x-ray. Thank god it was not so, it was just too high and they had to push down on my belly to bring it down, the whole time I was in a lot of pain and I thought my back would split open.

After some time, which felt like an eternity I gave birth to a baby boy, I was relieved when it was over.

When they told Jack that he had a son he was so very proud, and he said I must get cigars. I did not know what he meant but I was told that's what a new father does!

We named the baby Michael John and we were so happy to be finally parents!

Another one of my dreams came true!

Jack's father was the first one to see his new grandson because he was in the same hospital and the nurse took him to the baby station!

Soon after my father-in-law was transferred to a hospital to New York and exactly three months after our son was born, he died. It was very hard for all of us he was only 68 years old, he was such a good man!

Our son gave us so much joy and he was a good baby, he grew up fast. Rene and I talked about making my mother come for a visit and Jack's brother Mike sent her an open ticket. When our son Michael was one year old, my mother came for the first time to America.

She stayed with my sister Rene, who lived now very close to us. She came by herself and that was great, we did not have to deal with my stepfather. We took her lots of places and showed her as much as we could. She was only going to stay one month but we did not want her to go home so we extended her stay for another month and she loved it even though her husband gave her a hard time.

We knew she never been any where special and we wanted to show her as much as we could. Jack and I drove with her to Washington, DC and as we visited the capital one of the senator's shook hands with her and she got so excited and she believed she was someone special that he did that.

We tried to spoil her and give her the best time ever!

In 1969 we purchased a house on Long Island, NY. We wanted to give our son more space and a yard to play in!

This was another dream of mine to someday own a house!

In January of 1971 we welcomed our second son and named him Paul!

Our children gave us much joy as they grew up! During our

years of marriage, we enjoyed traveling a lot! Because of Jack's job we were able to do just that, and we took advantage of it.

I always wanted to travel back to east Germany and find out what happened to the family I stayed with when I was a child. It was now possible because the border wall was no longer standing between east and west Germany.

So, my husband and I decided to go there and try to locate them. We first flew into Berlin, Germany in 1994 and visited the city for a few days. Then we drove to Dresden and I was amazed, how they build up this city. The church which was almost destroyed was built up again with all the same stones and brick's they had saved and marked. It was beautiful; I couldn't believe what they had accomplished.

From there we drove into the little town of Ottendorf- Okrilla. We stopped a gentleman on the road and showed him the pictures I had from the family and asked him if by any chance he recognized anyone. To my surprise he did and told me that the older daughter Gitta went to school with him and she still lives in the same house. I did not recall the name of the street, but as soon as he told me I remembered. He told me he would call her to see if she would like to see me.

She said yes and he took us there. As soon as I saw Gitta I recognized her, and I became very emotional.

She invited us in and as soon as I stepped into the house, I knew every room and Gitta was surprised of how much I remembered. She told me all about her parents who had died some years ago and she said that her sister Ingrid lived in Berlin. She also informed me that her father was a SS Nazi officer in the German army, that is why he couldn't tell me where they were moving to, but they only went to Berlin where the headquarters were.

I would, have never guessed that, he was a very loving man!

She called her sister in Berlin and told her who I was. Ingrid wanted to talk to me and when we did, she invited me to come and see her the next time I am in Germany. We flew there in 1995 and when I saw her at the airport, I knew her immediately, even after 40 years. We had a lot to talk about and she told me what a change it was now, since Germany united. I said to her that when I was a child and stayed with them, it was the only nice memory I had of my childhood and I would like to invite them to my house to give something back.

Ingrid and her husband Lutz came to visit us when we lived already in Las Vegas and we showed them us much as we could. We are still staying in touch, but her sister Gitta died a few years ago!

Chapter 48

EVEN THOUGH WE also had some hardships during our years together, I could not have wished for a better Life!

My mother passed away in November 2001 and I went to Germany to be with her in her last weeks of her life.

Jack and I worked hard and looked forward for our retirement and in 2002 when the time came, we moved to Henderson (Las Vegas), Nevada.

In 2008 we were made grandparents by my son Michael and daughter-in-law Patricia with a little girl named Madison. She is the light of my life.

In 2015 we celebrated our 50. Golden anniversary and took our children on a cruise to celebrate and in July we flew to Germany and had a big party with my German family!

I guess when you wish hard enough , all your dreams can come true!

CPSIA information can be obtained
at www.ICGtesting.com
Printed in the USA
BVHW031730250520
580288BV00001B/153